Collins

German

phrasebook

Consultant
Marieke O'Connor

First published 1993
This edition published 2007
Copyright © HarperCollins Publishers
Reprint 10 9 8 7 6 5 4 3 2 1
Typeset by Davidson Pre-Press, Glasgow
Printed in Malaysia by Imago

www.collinslanguage.com
ISBN 13 978-0-00-724669-4
ISBN 10 0-00-724669-2

Using your phrasebook

Your *Collins Gem Phrasebook* is designed to help you locate the exact phrase you need, when you need it, whether on holiday or for business. If you want to adapt the phrases, you can easily see where to substitute your own words using the dictionary section, and the clear, full-colour layout gives you direct access to the different topics.

The Gem Phrasebook includes:
- Over 70 topics arranged thematically. Each phrase is accompanied by a simple pronunciation guide which eliminates any problems pronouncing foreign words.

- A Top ten tips section to safeguard against any cultural faux pas, giving essential dos and don'ts for situations involving local customs or etiquette.

- Practical hints to make your stay trouble free, showing you where to go and what to do when dealing with everyday matters such as travel or hotels and offering valuable tourist information.

- Face to face sections so that you understand what it is being said to you. These example mini-dialogues give you a good idea of what to expect from a real conversation.

- Common announcements and messages you may hear, ensuring that you never miss the important information you need to know when out and about.

- A clearly laid-out 3000-word dictionary means you will never be stuck for words.

- A basic grammar section which will enable you to build on your phrases.

- A list of public holidays to avoid being caught out by unexpected opening and closing hours, and to make sure you don't miss the celebrations!

It's worth spending time before you embark on your travels just looking through the topics to see what is covered and becoming familiar with what might be said to you.

Whatever the situation, your *Gem Phrasebook* is sure to help!

Contents

Pronouncing German

In this book you are given the pronunciation of the phrases so that you will soon be able to recognize the different sounds. (The stressed syllable is marked in **bold**). Here are a few rules you should know:

German	sounds like	example	pronunciation
a	c**u**p/f**a**ther	das/Abend	das/**ah**bent
e	b**e**d/h**ai**r	Bett/Meer	bet/m**eh**r
o	n**o**t/r**oa**d	oft/rot	**o**ft/r**oh**t
u	p**u**t/b**oo**t	Nummer/gut	n**oo**mmer/g**oo**t
ai/ay	p**ie**	Mai/Mayer	my/my-er
au	n**ow**	Auto	**ow**toh
ei/ey	p**ie**	eine/Meyer	**y**n-e/my-er
eu	t**oy**	neun	n**oyn**
ie	k**ee**p	sie	zee
ch	lo**ch**	wach	va**kh**
j	**y**es	jagen	**y**ahgen
qu	dar**k v**iolet	Quittung	**kv**itt**oo**ng
s	**d**re**ss**	es	es
	di**zz**y	sie	**z**ee
	ship	sprechen	**sh**prekh-en
ß	**j**uice	Fuß	foos
th	**t**ea	Theater	**t**eh-ahter
v	**f**an	von	**f**on
w	**v**an	wir	**v**eer
z	pe**ts**	Zimmer	**ts**immer

Umlauts

German	sounds like	example	pronunciation
Ä	bed/hair	hätte/spät	het-e/shpeht
ÄU	boy	läutet	loytet
Ö	Arthur/fur	können/Höhe	kur'nen/hur'-e*
Ü	duke/due	dürfen/Mühe	duerfen/mue-e

* **ur'** as in *hurt* without the **r** pronounced

A final **e** is always pronounced, but weakly like the *e* in *the*: **Seide** (**zy**-de), **bitte** (**bit**-e).

An underline indicates a short vowel, e.g. **Mutter** (**moo**tter), **Mörder** (**mur**der), **Küste** (**kue**ste). If an **h** is added after the vowel, the sound is longer, e.g. **Tag** (t**ah**k), **Mädchen** (m**eh**t-khen), **Leben** (**leh**ben), **hoch** (h**oh**kh).

Top ten tips

1 Try not to put your hands on your lap while eating, as to the Germans this looks as if you are giving the food to the dog!

2 If someone holds an academic title it's always polite to use it.

3 When introduced to an adult, address them by their title and surname until they suggest using first names.

4 If your conversation partner sneezes, say '**Gesundheit**' (bless you!).

5 Shake hands when you get introduced to an adult.

6 In restaurants in general, wait until everyone is served before you dig in, and say '**Guten Appetit!**' before you start. The latter is not entirely necessary, but considered good form.

7 Always use the polite '**Sie**' form, except with friends and colleagues of your own age.

8   When asked '**Wie geht es Ihnen?**' you should
    respond by first thanking them, saying '**Danke,
    gut**'.

9   Answer the phone by using your surname:
    '**Bader, hallo**'; if you're at work, then follow this
    with the name of your company.

10 Sundays are sacred. It's the '**Ruhe Tag**' so you
    should be aware that noise is kept to a
    minimum.

Talking to people

Hello/goodbye, yes/no

When Germans meet they generally shake hands.
The words for Mr and Mrs are **Herr** and **Frau**. Note
that **Fräulein** (Miss) is no longer used, as it sounds
rather patronising.

Please/Don't mention it	**Bitte**	
	bit-e	
Thanks (very much)	**Danke schön**	
	dang-ke shur'n	
Yes	**Ja**	
	yah	
No	**Nein**	
	nyn	
OK!	**Ok!**	
	o**kay**!	
Sir/Mr	**Herr**	
	her	
Madam/Mrs/Ms	**Frau**	
	frow	

Miss (rarely used nowadays)	**Fräulein**
	froylyn
Hello	**Guten Tag**
	gooten **tahk**
Hi	**Hallo**
	hal**loh**
Goodbye	**Auf Wiedersehen**
	owf **vee**der-zehn
Bye	**Tschüss**
	tshues
See you later	**Bis später**
	bis **shpeh**ter
See you tomorrow	**Bis morgen**
	bis **mor**gen
Good morning	**Guten Morgen**
	gooten **mor**gen
Good evening	**Guten Abend**
	gooten **ah**bent
Goodnight	**Gute Nacht**
	goote **nakht**
Excuse me!/Sorry!	**Entschuldigung!**
	ent**shool**di-goong!
Pardon?	**Wie, bitte?**
	vee **bit**-e?
How are you?	**Wie geht es Ihnen?**
	vee geht es **ee**nen?
Fine, thanks	**Danke, gut**
	dang-ke, **goot**

12

And you?	**Und Ihnen?**
	oont **ee**nen?
I don't speak German	**Ich spreche kein Deutsch**
	ikh **shpre**-khe kyn doytsh
Do you speak English?	**Sprechen Sie Englisch?**
	shprekh-en zee **eng**-lish?

Key phrases

• •

You don't need to say complicated things to get what you want. Often simply naming the thing and adding **bitte** will do the trick.

the (masculine)	**der/den**
	dehr/dehn
(feminine)	**die**
	dee
(neuter)	**das**
	das
(plural)	**die**
	dee
the station	**der Bahnhof**
	dehr **bahn**-hohf
the shops	**die Geschäfte**
	dee ge**shef**-te

a/one (masculine)	**ein/einen**
	yn/**yn**-en
(feminine)	**eine**
	yn-e
(neuter)	**ein**
	yn
a ticket	**eine Fahrkarte**
	yn-e **fahr**kar-te
one stamp	**eine Briefmarke**
	yn-e **breef**mar-ke
a room	**ein Zimmer**
	yn **tsimm**er
one bottle	**eine Flasche**
	yn-e **flash**-e
some (uncountable)	**etwas...**
	etvas...
(countable)	**ein paar...**
	yn pahr...
some sugar	**etwas Zucker**
	etvas **tsoo**ker
some jam	**etwas Marmelade**
	etvas mar-me-**lah**-de
some cherries	**ein paar Kirschen**
	yn pahr **kir**shen
Do you have a room?	**Haben Sie ein Zimmer frei?**
	hahben zee yn **tsimm**er fry?
Do you have some milk?	**Haben Sie etwas Milch?**
	hahben zee **et**vas milkh?

I'd like...	**Ich möchte...**	
	ikh **mur'kh**-te...	
We'd like...	**Wir möchten...**	
	veer **mur'kh**ten...	
Some more...	**Etwas mehr...**	
	etvas mehr...	
Another...	**Noch ein/eine...**	
	nokh yn/**yn**-e...	
Some more bread	**Etwas mehr Brot**	
	etvas mehr **broht**	
Some more glasses	**Noch ein paar Gläser**	
	nokh yn pahr **gleh**zer	
Another coffee	**Noch einen Kaffee**	
	nokh **yn**-en ka**feh**	
Another beer	**Noch ein Bier**	
	nokh yn beer	
How much is it?	**Was kostet das?**	
	vas **kos**tet das?	
How much is the room?	**Was kostet das Zimmer?**	
	vas **kos**tet das **tsimm**er?	
large/small	**groß/klein**	
	grohs/klyn	
with/without	**mit/ohne**	
	mit/**oh**-ne	
Where is/are...?	**Wo ist/sind...?**	
	vo ist/sint...?	
the nearest...	**der/die/das nächste...**	
	dehr/dee/das **neh**-kste...	

15

How do I get...?	**Wie komme ich...?**	vee **kom**-e ikh...?
to the station	**zum Bahnhof**	ts**oo**m **bahn**-hohf
to the bar	**zur Bar**	tsoor bar
to Berlin	**nach Berlin**	nahkh ber**leen**
There is/are...	**Es gibt...**	es gipt...
There isn't/ aren't any...	**Es gibt keine...**	es gipt **kyn**-e...
When...?	**Wann...?**	van...?
At what time...?	**Um wie viel Uhr...?**	<u>oo</u>m vee feel oo-er...?
today	**heute**	**hoy**-te
tomorrow	**morgen**	**mor**gen
Can I...?	**Kann ich...?**	kan ikh...?
smoke here	**hier rauchen**	heer **row**-khen
taste it	**es probieren**	es pro-**beer**-ren

Signs and notices

Eingang	entrance
Ausgang	exit
geöffnet	open
geschlossen	closed
heiß	hot
kalt	cold
Trinkwasser	drinking water
ziehen	pull
drücken	push
rechts	right
links	left
bitte...	please...
zum Mitnehmen	take-away
frei	free, vacant
besetzt	engaged
Selbstbedienung	self-service
Herren	gents
Damen	ladies
außer Betrieb	out of order
Kasse	cash desk
Baden verboten	no bathing
zu vermieten	for hire/to rent
zu verkaufen	for sale
Ausverkauf	sale
Untergeschoss	basement

Erdgeschoss	ground floor
Aufzug	lift
klingeln	ring
drücken	press
privat	private
Zimmer frei	rooms available
belegt	no vacancies
Notausgang	emergency exit
Fahrkarten	tickets
zu den Zügen	to the trains
bitte wählen Sie	please select
zahlbar mit	pay with
Reisezentrum	travel centre
Fahrkarte entwerten	validate your ticket
Gepäckaufbewahrung	left luggage
Fahrplan	timetable
Abfahrt (AB)	departure
Ankunft (AN)	arrival
Gleis	platform
Nichtraucher	non-smoking
Raucher	smoking
Rauchen verboten	no smoking

Polite expressions

There are two forms of address in German, formal (**Sie**) and informal (**du**). You should always stick to the formal until you are invited to **duzen** (to use the informal **du**).

The meal was delicious	**Das Essen war köstlich** das **ess**en var **kur'st**likh
Thank you very much	**Vielen Dank** **fee**len dank
You are very kind	**Das ist sehr nett von Ihnen** das ist zehr net fon **ee**nen
Delighted to meet you	**Freut mich, Sie kennenzulernen** froyt mikh, zee **kenn**en-tsoo-**ler**nen

Celebrations

I'd like to wish you...	**Ich wünsche Ihnen/dir...** ikh **vuen**-she **ee**nen/deer...
Merry Christmas!	**Frohe Weihnachten!** **froh**-e **vy**-nakhten!
Happy New Year!	**Ein frohes neues Jahr!** yn **froh**-es **noy**-es yahr!

19

All the best!	**Alles Gute!**
	al-es **goo**-te!
Happy birthday!	**Herzlichen Glückwunsch**
	zum Geburtstag!
	herts-likhen **gluek**-voonsh
	ts<u>oo</u>m ge-**boorts**-tahk!
Have a good trip!	**Gute Reise!**
	goo-te **ry**-ze!
Cheers!	**Prost!** or **Prosit!**
	prohst/**proh**zit!
To your health!	**Zum Wohl!**
	ts<u>oo</u>m vohl!

Making friends

· ·

We have used the informal **du** form for these conversations.

FACE TO FACE

A **Wie heißt du?**
vee hyst doo?
What's your name?

B **Ich heiße...**
ikh **hy**-se...
My name is...

A Woher kommst du?
voh-**her** komst doo?
Where are you from?

B Ich komme aus Großbritannien
ikh **kom**-e ows grohs-bri-**ta**-ni-en
I'm British (I come from...Britain)

A Sehr erfreut!
zehr er**froyt**!
Pleased to meet you!

How old are you?	**Wie alt bist du?**
	vee alt bist doo?
I'm ... years old	**Ich bin ... Jahre alt**
	ikh bin ... **yah**-re alt
Where do you live?	**Wo wohnst du?**
	voh vohnst doo?
Where do you live? (plural)	**Wo wohnt ihr?**
	voh vohnt eer?
I live in London	**Ich wohne in London**
	ikh **voh**-ne in **lon**don
We live in Glasgow	**Wir wohnen in Glasgow**
	veer **voh**nen in **glahs**goh
I'm still studying	**Ich studiere noch**
	ikh sht<u>oo</u>-**deer**-re nokh
I work	**Ich arbeite**
	ikh **ar**by-te
I'm retired	**Ich bin pensioniert**
	ikh bin penzio-**neert**

Making friends

21

I'm...	**Ich bin...**
	ikh bin...
(not) married	**(nicht) verheiratet**
	(nikht) fer-**hy**-rahtet
divorced	**geschieden**
	ge-**shee**den
a widow(er)	**Witwe(r)**
	vit-ve(r)
I have .../	**Ich habe .../keine Kinder**
no children	ikh **hah**-be .../**kyn**-e **kin**der
I'm here on	**Ich bin hier auf Urlaub**
holiday	ikh bin heer owf **oor**lowp
I'm here on	**Ich bin geschäftlich hier**
business	ikh bin ge**sheft**likh heer
What work do	**Was machen Sie beruflich?**
you do?	vas **makh**en zee be-**roof**likh?
Do you enjoy it?	**Macht es Ihnen Spaß?**
	makht es **ee**nen shpahs?
I'm...	**Ich bin...**
	ikh bin...
a teacher	**Lehrer(in)**
	lehrer(in)
a manager	**Manager(in)**
	men-ed-zher(in)
I'm self-employed	**Ich bin selbstständig**
	ikh bin **zelbst**-shten-dikh

Weather

••

sonnig zonnikh	sunny
heiter hyter	fair
bewölkt be-**vur'lkt**	cloudy
regnerisch rehg-nerish	showery
Gewitter ge**vitt**er	thunderstorms
windig vindikh	windy
trocken trokken	dry

What is the weather forecast?	**Wie ist der Wetterbericht?**
	vee ist dehr **vett**er-berikht?
It's sunny	**Es ist sonnig**
	es ist **zonn**ikh
It's raining	**Es regnet**
	es **rehg**net
It's snowing	**Es schneit**
	es shnyt
It's windy	**Es ist windig**
	es ist **vin**dikh
What a lovely day!	**Was für ein herrlicher Tag!**
	vas fuer yn **her**-likh-er tahk!
What awful weather!	**Was für ein Mistwetter!**
	vas fuer yn **mist**vetter!
What will the weather be like tomorrow?	**Wie wird das Wetter morgen?**
	vee virt das **vett**er **mor**gen?
It's very hot/cold	**Es ist sehr heiß/kalt**
	es ist zehr hys/kalt

23

Getting around

Asking the way

....

gegenüber **geh**gen-**ue**ber	opposite
neben **neh**ben	next to
in der Nähe von in dehr **neh**-e fon	near to
die Ampel dee **am**pel	traffic lights
an der Ecke an dehr **ek**-e	at the corner

FACE TO FACE

A **Entschuldigung! Wie komme ich zum Bahnhof?**
ent**shool**di-goong! vee **kom**-e ikh ts<u>oo</u>m **bahn**-hof?
Excuse me! How do I get to the station?

B **Immer geradeaus. Biegen Sie links ab nach der Kirche**
immer grah-de-**ows**. **bee**gen zee links ap nahkh dehr **kir**-khe
Straight on. Turn left after the church

A Ist es weit?
ist es vyt?
Is it far?

B Nein, fünf Minuten
nyn, fuenf mi**noo**ten
No, five minutes

We're looking for...	**Wir suchen...**
	veer **zoo**-khen...
Can I walk there?	**Kann ich dahin laufen?**
	kan ikh da**hin low**fen?
Is this the right way to...?	**Bin ich hier richtig zum/zur/ nach...?**
	bin ikh heer **rikh**-tikh ts<u>oo</u>m/ ts<u>oo</u>r/nahkh...?
How do I get onto the motorway?	**Wie komme ich zur Autobahn?**
	vee **kom**-e ikh tsoor **ow**toh-bahn?
Can you show me on the map?	**Können Sie mir das auf der Karte zeigen?**
	kur'nen zee meer das owf dehr **kar**-te **tsy**gen?

Bus and coach

If you are planning to use public transport, you can buy a multiple ticket – **eine Mehrfahrtenkarte**. You have to stamp it either on board the bus/tram/underground or at the bus stop. Other options are **eine Touristenkarte** (tourist pass) or **eine Familienkarte** (family ticket).

FACE TO FACE

A **Entschuldigung, gibt es einen Bus nach Bonn?**
ent**shool**di-goong, gipt es **yn**-en boos nahkh bon?
Is there a bus to Bonn?

B **Ja, die Nummer 15**
yah, dee noommer **fuenf**-tsehn
Yes, number 15

A **Wo fährt der Bus ab?**
voh fehrt dehr boos ap?
Where does the bus leave from?

B **Neben dem Museum**
nehben dehm moo-**zeh**-oom
Next to the museum

> **Luggage** (p 84)

A **Wo kann ich Fahrscheine kaufen?**
voh kann ikh **fahr**-shyn-e **kow**fen?
Where can I buy tickets?

B **Im Bus**
im <u>boos</u>
On the bus

How much is it to...?	**Was kostet es bis zum/zur/ nach...?**
	vas **kos**tet es bis ts<u>oo</u>m/ts<u>oo</u>r/ nahkh...?
How often are the buses/trams to...?	**Wie oft fahren die Busse/ Straßenbahnen zum/zur/ nach...?**
	vee oft **fah**ren dee **boos**-e/ **shtrah**-sen-bahnen ts<u>oo</u>m/ tsoor/nahkh...?
Please tell me when to get off	**Sagen Sie mir bitte, wann ich aussteigen muss**
	zahgen zee meer **bit**-e, van ikh **ows**-shtygen m<u>oo</u>s
Please let me off	**Kann ich bitte aussteigen?**
	kan ikh **bit**-e **ows**-shtygen?
This is my stop	**Das ist meine Haltestelle**
	das ist **myn**-e **hal**-te-shtel-e

Metro

Most German cities operate an integrated transport system. Tickets cover bus, **U-Bahn** (metro) and **S-Bahn** (suburban trains).

Where is the nearest metro station?	**Wo ist die nächste U-Bahn-Haltestelle?** voh ist dee **neh**-kste **oo**-bahn-**hal**-te-shtel-e?
How does the ticket machine work?	**Wie funktioniert der Automat?** vee <u>foo</u>nk-tsio-**neert** dehr owtoh-**maht**?
I'm going to...	**Ich möchte nach...** ikh **mur'kh**-te nahkh...
Do you have a transport map?	**Gibt es eine Übersichtskarte für den Nahverkehr?** gipt es **yn**-e ueber-zikhts-**kar**-te fuer den **nah**-ferkehr?
How do I get to...?	**Wie komme ich nach...?** vee **kom**-e ikh nahkh...?
Do I have to change?	**Muss ich umsteigen?** m<u>oo</u>s ikh **oom**-shtygen?
Where?	**Wo?** voh?
Which line is it for...?	**Welche Linie fährt nach...?** **vel**-khe **lee**-nee-e fehrt nahkh...?

Getting around

28

In which direction?	**In welche Richtung?**
	in **vel**-khe **rikh**-toong?
What is the next stop?	**Was ist der nächste Halt?**
	vas ist dehr **neh**-kste halt?
May I get past?	**Darf ich mal vorbei, bitte?**
	darf ikh mahl for**by** bit-e?
I have to get out here	**Ich muss hier aussteigen**
	ikh moos heer **ows**-shtygen

YOU MAY HEAR...

Für welche Zonen?	For which zones?
fuer **vel**-khe **tsoh**nen?	
Für die Innenstadt?	For the city centre?
fuer dee **in**-en-shtat?	

Train

Be sure to check if there is a supplement, **ein Zuschlag**, to pay before you board the train. It costs less if you buy it with your ticket. The ticket and information office are marked **Reisezentrum**.

> **Luggage** (p 84)

der Bahnhof	station
dehr **bahn**-hohf	
der Hauptbahnhof (Hbf)	main station
dehr **howpt**-bahn-hohf	
der Fahrplan	timetable
dehr **fahr**plahn	
die Abfahrt dee **ap**fahrt	departure
die Ankunft dee **an**<u>koo</u>nft	arrival

FACE TO FACE

A **Zwei Rückfahrkarten nach Berlin, bitte**
tsvy **ruek**-fahr-kahrten nahkh **ber**-leen, **bit**-e
Two return tickets to Berlin, please

B **Raucher oder Nichtraucher?**
row-kher ohder **nikht**-row-kher?
Smoking or non-smoking?

A **Nichtraucher, bitte, und zweiter Klasse**
nikht-row-kher, **bit**-e <u>oo</u>nt **tsvy**ter **klas**-e
Non-smoking, please, and 2nd class

B **Dreißig Euro, bitte**
dry-sikh **oy**roh, **bit**-e
Thirty euros, please

A **Wann geht der nächste Zug?**
van geht dehr **neh**-kste tzook?
When is the next train?

B **Um zehn Uhr**
<u>oo</u>m tsehn oo-er
At 10 o'clock

30

A single to...	**Einmal einfach nach...** **yn**-mahl **yn**-fakh nahkh...
Is there a supplement to pay?	**Muss ich einen Zuschlag zahlen?** moos ikh **yn**-en **tsoo**shlahk **tsah**len?
When does it arrive in...?	**Wann kommt er in ... an?** van komt ehr in ... an?
Do I need to change?	**Muss ich umsteigen?** moos ikh **oom**-shtygen?
Where?	**Wo?** voh?
How long is there to change trains?	**Wie viel Zeit habe ich zum Umsteigen?** vee feel tsyt **hah**-be ikh tsoom **oom**-shtygen?
Will my connecting train wait?	**Wartet der Anschlusszug?** **var**tet dehr **an**-shloos-tsook?
Which platform does it leave from?	**Von welchem Bahnsteig fährt er ab?** fon **vel**-khem **bahn**-shtyk fehrt ehr ap?
Does the train to ... leave from here?	**Fährt hier der Zug nach ... ab?** fehrt heer dehr tsook nahkh ... ap?
Is this the train for...?	**Ist das der Zug nach...?** ist das dehr tsook nahkh...?
When will it leave?	**Wann fährt er ab?** van fehrt ehr ap?

Does the train stop at...?	**Hält der Zug in...?** helt dehr tsook in...?
Please let me know when we get to...	**Bitte sagen Sie mir, wann wir in ... ankommen** **bit**-e **zah**gen zee meer, van veer in ... **an**kommen
Is this free? (seat)	**Ist hier noch frei?** ist heer nokh fry?
This is my seat	**Das ist mein Platz** das ist myn plats

YOU MAY HEAR...

Fahrscheine bitte **fahr**-shy-ne **bit**-e	Tickets please

Taxi

In Germany it is practically impossible to flag down a taxi in the street. You have to find a taxi rank, **Taxistand**, or phone for a taxi. You can often find adverts for taxi firms in public telephone boxes, and you must give your name and the address of the phone box, which will be written under the word **Standort**.

I want a taxi	**Ich hätte gern ein Taxi**	
	ikh **het**-e gern yn **ta**xi	
Where can I get a taxi?	**Wo bekomme ich hier ein Taxi?**	
	voh be-**kom**-e ikh heer yn **ta**xi?	
Please order me a taxi	**Bitte bestellen Sie mir ein Taxi**	
	bit-e be-**shtell**en zee meer yn **ta**xi	
straightaway	**sofort**	
	zoh**fort**	
for (time)	**für ... Uhr**	
	fuer ... oo-er	
My name is...	**Ich heiße...**	
	ikh **hy**-se...	
The address is...	**Die Adresse ist...**	
	dee a-**dres**-e ist...	
How much is it...?	**Was kostet die Fahrt ...?**	
	vas **kos**tet dee fahrt...?	
to the centre	**ins Zentrum**	
	ins **tsen**tr<u>oo</u>m	
to the station	**zum Bahnhof**	
	ts<u>oo</u>m **bahn**-hohf	
to the airport	**zum Flughafen**	
	ts<u>oo</u>m **flook**-hahfen	
to this address	**zu dieser Adresse**	
	tsoo **dee**zer a-**dres**-e	
How much is it?	**Was kostet das?**	
	vas **kos**tet das?	

Taxi

33

I need a receipt	**Ich brauche eine Quittung**
	ikh **brow**-khe **yn**-e **kvitt<u>oo</u>**ng
I'm in a hurry	**Ich habe es sehr eilig**
	ikh **hah**-be es zehr **y**-likh
Is it far?	**Ist es weit?**
	ist es vyt?

Boat and ferry

. . . .

When is the next boat/the next ferry to...?	**Wann fährt das nächste Schiff/die nächste Fähre nach ... ab?**
	van fehrt das **neh**-kste shif/ dee **neh**-kste **feh**-re nahkh... ap?
Is there a timetable?	**Gibt es einen Fahrplan?**
	gipt es **yn**-en **fahr**-plahn?
Is there a car ferry to...?	**Gibt es eine Autofähre nach...?**
	gipt es **yn**-e **ow**toh-feh-re nahkh...?
How much is...?	**Was kostet...?**
	vas **kos**tet...?
a single	**die einfache Fahrt**
	dee **yn**-fakh-e fahrt
a return	**eine Rückfahrkarte**
	yn-e **ruek**-fahr-kar-te

a tourist ticket	**eine Touristenkarte**
	yn-e too**ris**ten-kar-te
a family card	**eine Familienkarte**
	yn-e fa-**mee**li-en-kar-te
How much is it for a car and ... people?	**Was kostet es für ein Auto mit ... Personen?**
	vas **kos**tet es fuer yn **ow**toh mit ... per-**zoh**nen?
When is the first/ last boat?	**Wann geht das erste/letzte Schiff?**
	van geht das **ehr**-ste/**lets**-te shif?

YOU MAY HEAR...

| **Wollen Sie heute noch zurück?** | Do you want to come back today? |
| **vol**len zee **hoy**-te nokh tsoo**ruek**? | |

Air travel

. . . .

To the airport, please	**Zum Flughafen, bitte**
	tsoom **flook**-hahfen, **bit**-e
How do I get to (name town)?	**Wie komme ich nach...?**
	vee **kom**-e ikh nahkh...?

> **Luggage** (p 84)

How much is a taxi...?	**Wie viel kostet ein Taxi...?**
	vee feel **kos**tet yn **ta**xi...?
into town	**in die Stadt**
	in dee shtat
to the hotel	**zum Hotel**
	tsoom ho**tel**
Is there an airport bus to the city centre?	**Gibt es einen Airport-Bus zum Stadtzentrum?**
	gipt es **yn**-en **air**port-boos tsoom **shtat**-tsentroom?
Where do I check in for (airline)?	**Wo ist der Check-in für...?**
	voh ist dehr **check**-in fuer...?
Which is the departure gate for the flight to...?	**Welches Gate hat der Flug nach...?**
	vel-khes geht hat dehr flook nahkh...?
Where is the luggage for the flight from...?	**Wo ist das Gepäck vom Flug aus...?**
	voh ist das ge**pek** fom flook ows...?

YOU MAY HEAR...

Sie steigen am Gate Nummer ... ein	Boarding will take place at gate number...
zee **shty**gen am geht **noo**mmer ... yn	

Gehen Sie sofort zu Gate Nummer... **geh**en zee zoh**fort** tsoo geht **noo**mmer...	Go immediately to gate number...
Ihr Flug hat Verspätung eer flook hat fer-**shpeh**toong	Your flight is delayed

Customs control

••

With the Single European Market, European Union (EU) citizens are subject only to spot checks and can go through the blue customs channel when arriving from another EU country. There is no restriction on goods purchased by travellers in another EU country, provided they are **for personal use**.

die Passkontrolle dee **pas**-kontroll-e	passport control
der Zoll dehr tsoll	customs

I have a visa	**Ich habe ein Visum** ikh **hah**-be yn **vee**zoom

37

Driving

Car hire

der Führerschein dehr **fuer**-rer-shyn	driving licence
die Zulassung dee **tsoo**lass<u>oo</u>ng	log book

I want to hire a car	**Ich möchte ein Auto mieten** ikh **mur'kh**-te yn **ow**toh **mee**ten
for one day	**für einen Tag** fuer **yn**-en tahk
for ... days	**für ... Tage** fuer ... **tah**-ge
How much is the car...?	**Was kostet das Auto...?** vas **kos**tet das **ow**toh...?
per day	**pro Tag** proh tahk
per week	**pro Woche** proh **vokh**-e
How much is the deposit?	**Wie hoch ist die Kaution?** vee hohkh ist dee kow-**tsiohn**?

Is there a kilometre charge?	**Verlangen Sie eine Kilometergebühr?**
	ferlangen zee yn-e kiloh-mehter-gebuer?
How much is it?	**Wie hoch ist sie?**
	vee hohkh ist zee?
What is included in the insurance?	**Was ist alles in der Versicherung inbegriffen?**
	vas ist al-es in dehr ferzikher-roong inbegriffen?
Must I return the car here?	**Muss ich das Auto hierher zurückbringen?**
	moos ikh das owtoh heer-hehr tsooruek-bringen?
By what time?	**Bis wann?**
	bis van?
I'd like to leave it in...	**Ich würde es gern in ... abgeben**
	ikh vuer-de es gern in ... apgehben
What do I do if I...?	**Was mache ich...?**
	vas makhe ikh...?
break down	**bei einer Panne**
	by yn-er pan-e
have an accident	**bei einem Unfall**
	by yn-em oonfall

Car hire

39

Driving

Bitte bringen Sie das Auto voll betankt zurück bit-e **bring**en zee das **ow**toh fol be-**tankt** tsoo**ruek**	Please return the car with a full tank

Driving

• •

The speed limits in Germany are 50 km/h in built up areas and 100 km/h on ordinary roads. There is no speed restriction on motorways, though 130 km/h is recommended. But be careful: some sections do have restrictions and these are signposted. Most cities have controlled parking areas: watch out for **Zone** signs. You cannot park within these zones.

Is this the road to...?	**Ist das die Straße nach...?** ist das dee **shtrah**-se nahkh...?
Which junction is it for...?	**Welche Anschlussstelle führt nach...?** **vel**-khe **an**shloos-shtel-e fuert nahkh...?
Can I park here?	**Kann ich hier parken?** kan ikh heer **par**ken?
How long for?	**Für wie lange?** fuer vee **lang**-e?

Petrol

• •

Petrol is more expensive at motorway service
stations. An **Autohof** (a trucker stop) is a cheaper
alternative.

das Benzin	das ben**tseen**	petrol
bleifrei	**bly**fry	unleaded
das Öl	das ur'l	oil

Is there a petrol station near here?	**Ist hier in der Nähe eine Tankstelle?**
	ist heer in dehr **neh**-e **yn**-e **tank**-shtel-e?
Fill it up, please	**Voll tanken, bitte**
	fol **tang**ken, **bit**-e
Please check the oil/the water/ the tyre pressure	**Bitte überprüfen Sie das Öl/das Wasser/ den Reifendruck**
	bit-e ueber-**prue**fen zee das ur'l/ das **vass**er/den **ry**fen-drook
... euros worth of unleaded petrol	**Für ... Euro bleifrei bitte**
	fuer ... **oy**ro **bly**fry **bit**-e
Do you take this credit card?	**Nehmen Sie diese Kreditkarte?**
	nehmen zee **dee**-ze kre**dit**-kar-te?
Pump number...	**Säule Nummer...**
	zoy-le **noomm**er...

| Welche Säule? | Which pump? |
| **vel**-khe **zoy**-le? | |

Breakdown

....

If you break down on the German motorway, by law you should place a warning triangle 100 metres behind your vehicle.

Can you help me?	**Können Sie mir helfen?**
	kur'nen zee meer **hel**fen?
My car has broken down	**Ich habe eine Autopanne**
	ikh **hah**-be **yn**-e **ow**toh-pan-e
The car won't start	**Das Auto springt nicht an**
	das **ow**toh shpringt nikht an
I've run out of petrol	**Ich habe kein Benzin mehr**
	ikh **hah**-be kyn ben**tseen** mehr
Is there a garage near here?	**Ist eine Werkstatt in der Nähe?**
	ist **yn**-e **verk**shtat in dehr **neh**-e?
Can you tow me to the nearest garage?	**Könnten Sie mich bis zur nächsten Werkstatt abschleppen?**
	kur'nten zee mikh bis tsoor **neh**-ksten **verk**shtat **ap**shleppen?

Driving

42

Car parts

The ... doesn't work	**Der/Die/Das ... funktioniert nicht**
	dehr/dee/das ... foonk-tsio-**neert** nikht
The ... don't work	**Die ... funktionieren nicht**
	dee...foonk-tsio-**neer**-ren nikht

accelerator	**das Gaspedal**	**gahs**-pedahl
battery	**die Batterie**	ba-te-**ree**
brakes	**die Bremsen**	**brem**zen
central locking	**die Zentralver-riegelung**	tsen**trahl**-fer-**ree**-geloong
choke	**der Choke**	chohk
clutch	**die Kupplung**	**koop**loong
distributor	**der Verteiler**	fer**ty**ler
engine	**der Motor**	**moh**tor
exhaust pipe	**das Auspuffrohr**	**ows**poof-rohr
fanbelt	**der Keilriemen**	**kyl**reemen
fuse	**die Sicherung**	**zikh**er-**roong**
gears	**das Getriebe**	ge**tree**-be
handbrake	**die Handbremse**	**hant**-brem-ze
headlights	**die Scheinwerfer**	**shyn**-verfer
heating	**die Heizung**	**hyt**soong
ignition	**die Zündung**	**tsuen**doong
indicator	**der Blinker**	**bling**ker
points	**der Unterbrecher**	oonter-**brekh**-er

43

radiator	der Kühler	**kue**ler
rear lights	das Rücklicht	**ruek**likht
seat belt	der Sicherheits-gurt	**zikh**er-hyts-<u>goor</u>t
spare wheel	das Ersatzrad	er**zats**-raht
spark plugs	die Zündkerzen	**tsuent**-kertsen
steering	die Lenkung	**leng**-<u>koo</u>ng
tyre	der Reifen	**ry**fen
wheel	das Rad	raht
windscreen	die Windschutz-scheibe	**vint**-shoots-shy-be
windscreen wiper	der Scheiben-wischer	**shy**ben-visher

Road signs

sliding danger

road toll

police station

one way

emergency phone

North

West

East

South

bus stop

customs post

speed limits in
Germany are in km/h

Ausfahrt

exit

Berlin 2

directions to Autobahn

Umleitung

detour approach

Driving

Staying somewhere

Hotel (booking)

• •

You can book accommodation over the internet using the German tourist office website **www.deutschland-tourismus.de**.

FACE TO FACE

A **Ich möchte ein Einzel-/Doppelzimmer (buchen)**
ikh **mur'kh**-te yn **yn**tsel-/**dop**pel-**tsimm**er (**boo**-khen)
I'd like (to book) a single/double room

B **Für wie viele Nächte?**
für vee **fee**-le **nekh**-te?
For how many nights?

A **Wir möchten ... Nächte bleiben**
veer **mur'kh**ten ... **nekh**-te **bly**ben
We'd like to stay ... nights

B **Wie heißen Sie, bitte?**
vee **hy**-sen zee **bit**-e?
What is your name, please?

How much is it?	**Was kostet es?**
	vas **kos**tet es?
per night	**pro Nacht**
	proh nakht
per week	**pro Woche**
	proh **vokh**-e
from ... till ...	**vom ... bis zum ...**
	fom ... bis ts<u>oo</u>m ...
a twin-bedded room	**ein Zweibettzimmer**
	yn **tsvy**-bet-tsimmer
with bath	**mit Bad**
	mit baht
with shower	**mit Dusche**
	mit **doo**-she
with an extra bed for a child	**mit einem zusätzlichen Kinderbett**
	mit **yn**-em **tsoo**-zets-likhen **kin**derbet
How much is...?	**Was kostet...?**
	vas **kos**tet...?
half board	**Halbpension**
	halp-penziohn
full board	**Vollpension**
	fol-penziohn
Is breakfast included?	**Ist das Frühstück inbegriffen?**
	ist das **frue**shtuek **in**begriffen?
I'll arrive at ... o'clock	**Ich komme um ... Uhr an**
	ikh **kom**-e <u>oo</u>m ... <u>oo</u>-er an

Wir sind ausgebucht veer zint **ows**-gebookht	We're full
Für wie viele Nächte? fuer vee **fee**-le **nekh**-te?	For how many nights?
Bitte bestätigen Sie... **bit**-e be-**shteh**ti-gen zee...	Please confirm...
per E-Mail per **ee**-mehl	by email
per Fax per fax	by fax
Wann kommen Sie an? van **komm**en zee an?	What time will you arrive?
Wir brauchen Ihre Kreditkartennummer veer **brow**-khen **eer**-re kre**dit**-karten-noommer	We need your credit card number

Hotel desk

Hotel desk

• •

A **Hotel Garni** is a bed and breakfast. A **Gasthof** is
usually a pub or wine bar with a few guestrooms.
They are generally good value.

Have you any vacancies?	**Haben Sie Zimmer frei?** **hah**ben zee **tsimm**er fry?

49

for tonight	**für heute Nacht**	
	fuer **hoy**-te nakht	
for 2 nights	**für zwei Nächte**	
	fuer tsvy **nekh**-te	
Where can I park the car?	**Wo kann ich mein Auto parken?**	
	voh kan ich myn **ow**toh **par**ken?	
What time is...?	**Wann gibt es...?**	
	van gipt es...?	
dinner (evening)	**Abendessen**	
	ahbent-essen	
breakfast	**Frühstück**	
	frueshtuek	
The key, please	**Den Schlüssel, bitte**	
	dehn **shluess**el, **bit**-e	
Room number...	**Zimmer** (number)	
	tsimmer...	
I'm leaving tomorrow	**Ich reise morgen ab**	
	ikh **ry**-ze **mor**gen ap	
Please prepare the bill	**Machen Sie bitte die Rechnung fertig**	
	makhen zee **bit**-e dee **rekh**noong **fer**tikh	

Camping

••••••••••••••••••••••••••••••••

Information about campsites and their charges is
generally available from local tourist offices.

Do you have any vacancies?	**Haben Sie noch Plätze frei?**
	hahben zee nokh **plet**-se fry?
We'd like to stay for ... nights	**Wir möchten ... Nächte bleiben**
	veer **mur'kh**ten ... **nekh**-te **bly**ben
How much is it per night...?	**Was kostet die Nacht...?**
	vas **kos**tet dee nakht...?
for a tent	**pro Zelt**
	proh tselt
per person	**pro Person**
	proh per**zohn**
Are showers...	**Ist Duschen...**
	ist **doo**shen...
Is hot water...	**Ist Heißwasser...**
	ist hys-**vass**er...
Is electricity...	**Ist Strom...**
	ist shtrohm...
...included in the price?	**...im Preis inbegriffen?**
	...im prys **in**begriffen?
Is there a restaurant?	**Gibt es ein Restaurant?**
	gipt es yn restoh-**rant**?
Is there a shop?	**Gibt es einen Laden?**
	gipt es **yn**-en **lah**den?

Self-catering

Recycling in Germany is taken very seriously. Bins are colour-coded according to what can be put into them: brown is for biodegradable material, blue for paper, black for general waste and yellow for any packaging carrying the recycling symbol.

Who do we contact if there are problems?	**An wen können wir uns wenden, wenn wir ein Problem haben?** an **vehn kur'**nen veer oonts **ven**den ven veer yn prob**lehm hah**ben?
How does the heating work?	**Wie funktioniert die Heizung?** vee foonk-tsio-**neert** dee **hyt**soong?
Where is the nearest supermarket?	**Wo ist der nächste Supermarkt?** voh ist dehr **neh**-kste **zoo**permarkt?
Is there always hot water?	**Gibt es immer Heißwasser?** gipt es **imm**er **hys**-vasser?
Where do we leave the rubbish?	**Wo sollen wir den Müll entsorgen?** voh **zoll**en veer dehn m<u>ue</u>l ent**zorg**en?

> Sightseeing and tourist office (p 65)

Shopping

Shopping phrases

der Ausverkauf dehr **ows**ferkowf	sale
das Stück das sht<u>ue</u>k	single item

I'm looking for a present for my mother/a child — **Ich suche ein Geschenk für meine Mutter/ein Kind**
 ikh **zoo**-khe yn ge**shenk** fuer **myn**-e **moott**er/yn kint

It's too expensive for me — **Das ist mir zu teuer**
 das ist meer tsoo **toy**er

Do you have...? — **Haben Sie...?**
 hahben zee...?

Where is the nearest...? — **Wo ist der/die/das nächste...?**
 voh ist dehr/dee/das **neh**-kste...?

How do I get to the main shopping area? — **Wie komme ich zum Hauptgeschäftszentrum?**
 vee **kom**-e ikh ts<u>oo</u>m howpt-ge**shefts**-tsentr<u>oo</u>m?

53

Which floor are shoes on?	**Auf welchem Stockwerk sind die Schuhe?**
	owf **vel**-khem **shtok**verk zint dee **shoo**-e?
Have you anything else?	**Haben Sie noch etwas anderes?**
	hahben zee nokh **et**vas **an**-der-res?

YOU MAY HEAR...

Kann ich Ihnen helfen? kan ikh **ee**nen **hel**fen?	Can I help you?
Darf es sonst noch etwas sein? darf es zonst nokh **et**vas zyn?	Would you like anything else?

Shops

Most large shops in Germany are open all day, from about 9am to 6pm Monday to Friday. On Saturdays they are open until 4pm and there is late-night shopping on Thursdays until 8pm. Shops are shut on Sundays.

| baker's | **Bäckerei** | bek-e-**ry** |
| bookshop | **Buchhandlung** | **bookh**-hantl<u>oo</u>ng |

butcher's	**Fleischerei**	fly-she-**ry**
cake shop	**Konditorei**	kon-di-toh-**ry**
clothes	**Kleidung**	**kly**<u>doong</u>
department store	**Warenhaus**	**vah**ren-hows
dry-cleaner's	**Reinigung**	**ry**nig<u>oong</u>
gifts	**Geschenkartikel**	ge**shenk**-artikel
greengrocer's	**Gemüseladen**	ge**mue**-ze-**lah**den
grocer's	**Lebensmittel- laden**	**leh**bens-mittel-**lah**den
hairdresser's	**Friseur**	free**zur**
health food shop	**Reformhaus**	re**form**-hows
household (goods)	**Haushalts- waren**	**hows**-halts-vahren
hardware	**Eisenwaren- handlung**	**y**zen-vahren-**hant**<u>loong</u>
jeweller's	**Juwelier**	yoo-ve-**leer**
market	**Markt**	markt
pharmacy	**Apotheke**	apo-**teh**-ke
self-service	**Selbstbedienung**	**zelpst**-be**dee**n<u>oong</u>
shoe shop	**Schuhgeschäft**	**shoo**-gesheft
shop	**Laden**	**lah**den
sports shop	**Sportgeschäft**	**shport**-gesheft
stationer's	**Schreibwaren- handlung**	**shryp**-vahren-**hant**<u>loong</u>

55

supermarket	**Supermarkt**	**zoo**permarkt
tobacconist's	**tabakladen**	**tab**ak-lahden
toy shop	**spielwarenladen**	**shpeel**-vahren-**lah**den

Food (general)

biscuits	**die Kekse**	**kehk**-se
bread	**das Brot**	broht
bread (brown)	**das Vollkornbrot**	**fol**korn-broht
bread roll	**das Brötchen**	**brur't**-khen
butter	**die Butter**	**boot**ter
cheese	**der Käse**	**keh**-ze
coffee (instant)	**der Instantkaffee**	instant-ka**feh**
cream	**die Sahne**	**zah**-ne
crisps	**die Chips**	chips
eggs	**die Eier**	**y**-er
flour	**das Mehl**	mehl
ham	**der Schinken**	**shing**ken
herbal tea	**der Kräutertee**	**kroy**ter-teh
honey	**der Honig**	**hoh**nikh
jam	**die Marmelade**	mar-me-**lah**-de
margarine	**die Margarine**	marga-**ree**-ne
marmalade	**die Orangen- marmelade**	o**ran**zhen-mar- me-**lah**-de
milk	**die Milch**	milkh
mustard	**der Senf**	zenf

oil	das Öl	url
orange juice	der Orangensaft	o**ran**zhen-zaft
pasta	die Nudeln	**noo**deln
pepper	der Pfeffer	**pfeff**er
rice	der Reis	rys
saccharin	der Süßstoff	**zues**-shtof
salt	das Salz	zalts
sausage	die Wurst	voorst
stock cube	der Suppenwürfel	**zoopp**en-v<u>ue</u>rfel
sugar	der Zucker	**tsoo**ker
tea	der Tee	teh
tin of	die Dose	**doh**-ze
tomatoes	Tomaten	to**mah**ten
vinegar	der Essig	**ess**ikh
yoghurt	der Jogurt	**yoh**goort

Food (fruit and veg)

Fruit

apples	die Äpfel	**ep**fel
apricots	die Aprikosen	apri-**koh**zen
bananas	die Bananen	ba**nah**nen
cherries	die Kirschen	**kir**shen
grapefruit	die Grapefruit	**grape**fruit
grapes	die Trauben	**trow**ben
lemon	die Zitrone	tsi**troh**-ne

melon	die Melone	me**loh**-ne
nectarines	die Nektarinen	nekta-**ree**nen
oranges	die Orangen	o**ran**zhen
peaches	die Pfirsiche	**pfir**-zi-khe
pears	die Birnen	**bir**nen
pineapple	die Ananas	**ann**a-nas
plums	die Pflaumen	**pflow**men
raspberries	die Himbeeren	**him**-behren
strawberries	die Erdbeeren	**ert**-behren

Vegetables

asparagus	der Spargel	**shpar**gel
broccoli	der Brokkoli	**bro**kkoli
carrots	die Karotten	ka**rott**en
cauliflower	der Blumenkohl	**bloo**men-kohl
courgettes	die Zucchini	tsoo**kee**nee
French beans	die grünen Bohnen	**grue**nen **boh**nen
garlic	der Knoblauch	**knohp**-lowkh
leeks	der Lauch	lowkh
lettuce	der Kopfsalat	**kopf**-zalaht
mushrooms	die Pilze	**pil**tse
onions	die Zwiebeln	**tsvee**beln
peas	die Erbsen	**erp**sen
peppers	die Paprika	**pap**rika
potatoes	die Kartoffeln	kar**toff**eln
spinach	der Spinat	shpi**naht**
tomatoes	die Tomaten	to**mah**ten

> **Measurements and quantities** (p 103)

Clothes

women's sizes		men's suit sizes		shoe sizes			
UK	EU	UK	EU	UK	EU	UK	EU
8	36	36	46	2	35	7	41
10	38	38	48	3	36	8	42
12	40	40	50	4	37	9	43
14	42	42	52	5	38	10	44
16	44	44	54	6	39	11	45
18	46	46	56				

FACE TO FACE

A **Kann ich das anprobieren?**
kan ikh das **an**prob**ee**r-ren?
May I try this on?

B **Ja, bitte. Passt es?**
yah **bit**-e. past es?
Please do. Does it fit you?

A **Es ist zu groß/klein/teuer**
es ist tsoo grohs/klyn/**toy**er
It's too big/small/expensive

B **Welche Größe haben Sie?**
vel-khe **grur'**-se **hah**ben zee?
What size are you?

Clothes

59

Do you have this in size...?	**Haben Sie das in Größe...?**
	hahben zee das in **grur'**-se...?
bigger	**größer**
	grur'ser
smaller	**kleiner**
	klyner
I'm just looking	**Ich schaue mich nur um**
	ikh **show**-e mikh noor <u>oom</u>
I'll take it	**Ich nehme es**
	ikh **neh**-me es

Clothes (articles)

belt	**der Gürtel**	**guer**tel
blouse	**die Bluse**	**bloo**-ze
bra	**der BH**	beh-**hah**
coat	**der Mantel**	**man**tel
dress	**das Kleid**	klyt
fleece	**das Fleece**	flees
gloves	**die Handschuhe**	**hant**-shoo-e
hat	**der Hut**	hoot
jacket	**das Jackett**	dja**ket**
knickers	**der Slip**	slip
nightdress	**das Nachthemd**	**nakht**-hemt
pyjamas	**der Pyjama**	pue-**jah**-ma
raincoat	**der Regenmantel**	**reh**gen-**man**tel

> **Paying** (p 82) > **Numbers** (p 105)

sandals	die Sandalen	zan**dah**len
scarf (silk)	das Tuch	tookh
scarf (wool)	der Schal	shahl
shirt	das Hemd	hemt
shorts	die Shorts	shorts
skirt	der Rock	rok
slippers	die Pantoffeln	pan**toff**-eln
socks	die Socken	**zokk**en
suit (man's)	der Anzug	**an**tsook
suit (woman's)	das Kostüm	kos**tuem**
swimsuit	der Badeanzug	**bah**-de-**an**tsook
tie	die Krawatte	kra**vat**-e
tights	die Strumpfhose	**shtroompf**-hoh-ze
tracksuit	der Trainings-anzug	**trehn**ings-**an**tsook
trousers	die Hose	**hoh**-ze
underpants	die Unterhose	**oon**ter-hoh-ze
zip	der Reißverschluss	**rys**-fershl<u>oo</u>s

Maps and guides

• •

Large railway stations and airport bookshops usually stock English newspapers and books, but they can be very expensive.

Have you...?	**Haben Sie...?** **hah**ben zee...?
a map of the town	**einen Stadtplan** **yn**-en **shtat**plahn
a map of the region	**eine Karte der Umgebung** **yn**-e **kar**-te dehr <u>oo</u>m-**geh**boong
Can you show me where ... is on the map?	**Können Sie mir auf der Karte zeigen, wo ... ist?** **kur**'nen zee meer owf dehr **kar**-te **tsy**gen, voh ... ist?
Do you have a guide book/a leaflet in English?	**Gibt es einen Reiseführer/ eine Broschüre auf Englisch?** gipt es **yn**-en **ry**-ze-fuer-rer/**yn**-e bro-**shue**-re owf **eng**-lish?
Do you have any English newspapers/ books?	**Haben Sie englische Zeitungen/Bücher?** **hah**ben zee **eng**-lish-e **tsy**-<u>toon</u>gen/**bue**-kher?

Post office

. . . .

Main Post Offices are open all day (9am to 6pm) Monday to Friday and on Saturday mornings. A red dot on German postboxes indicates that there is a late/weekend collection.

 > **Sightseeing and tourist office** (p 65)

das Postamt/die Post das **post**amt/dee post	post office
der Briefkasten dehr **bref**kasten	postbox
die Briefmarken dee **bref**marken	stamps

Where is the nearest post office?	**Wo ist das nächste Postamt?** voh ist das **neh**-kste **post**amt?
When is it open?	**Wann hat es auf?** van hat es owf?
Is there a postbox near here?	**Ist hier ein Briefkasten in der Nähe?** ist heer yn **bref**kasten in dehr **neh**-e?
Where can I buy stamps?	**Wo bekomme ich Briefmarken?** voh be-**kom**-e ikh **bref**marken?
Stamps for ... postcards to Great Britain, please	**Briefmarken für ... Postkarten nach England, bitte** **bref**marken fuer ... **post**karten nahkh **eng**-lant, **bit**-e

YOU MAY HEAR...

Füllen Sie das bitte aus **fuell**en zee das **bit**-e ows	Fill in this form, please

Post office

> **Money** (p 81) > **Paying** (p 82)   63

Photos

●●●●●●●●●●●●●●●●●●●●●●●●●●●●●

Where can I buy a tape for this camcorder?
Wo kann ich ein Band für diesen Camcorder kaufen?
voh kan ikh yn bant fuer **dee**zen **cam**corder **kow**fen?

Have you got a battery/memory card for this camera?
Haben Sie eine Batterie/eine Speicherkarte für diesen Fotoapparat?
hahben zee **yn**-e batte**ree**/**yn**-e **shpy**kher-kar-te fuer **dee**-ze **foh**toh-apa-**raht**?

Would you take a picture of us, please?
Könnten Sie bitte ein Foto von uns machen?
kur'nten zee **bit**-e yn **foh**toh fon oons **makh**en?

YOU MAY HEAR...	
Matt oder Hochglanz? matt **oh**der **hohkh**-glants?	Matt or glossy?
Die Fotos sind um ... / am ... fertig dee **foh**tohs zint oom ... / am ... **fer**tikh	The photos will be ready at (time)/ on (day)

64

Leisure

Sightseeing and tourist office

Monday is not a good day for sightseeing in Germany, as most museums and art galleries close on Mondays.

Where is the tourist office?	**Wo ist die Touristeninformation?**
	voh ist dee too**rist**en-informa**tsiohn**?
We'd like to go to...	**Wir möchten nach...**
	veer **mur'kh**ten nahkh...
Are there any excursions?	**Gibt es Ausflugsfahrten?**
	gipt es **ows**flooks-**fahr**ten?
How much does it cost to get in?	**Was kostet der Eintritt?**
	vas **kos**tet dehr **yn**-trit?
Are there any reductions for...?	**Gibt es eine Ermäßigung für...?**
	gipt es **yn**-e er-**meh**si-<u>goong</u> fuer...?
children	**Kinder**
	kinder

65

students	**Studenten**
	shtoo**den**ten
unemployed	**Arbeitslose**
	arbyts-loh-ze
senior citizens	**Rentner**
	rentner

Music

. . . .

Where can I/we get tickets for the concert?	**Wo gibt es Karten für das Konzert?**
	voh gipt es **kar**ten fuer das kon**tsert**?
Where can I/we hear some classical music/ jazz?	**Wo kann man hier klassische Musik/Jazz hören?**
	voh kan man heer **klas**ish-e moo**zeek**/jazz **hur'**-ren?

Cinema

. . . .

Films are generally dubbed in Germany. New films are usually released on Thursdays and many cinemas offer a discount of up to 50% on the so-called **Kinotag** (cinema day), usually Tuesday.

> **Making friends** (p 20)

Leisure

What's on at the cinema?	**Was gibt es im Kino?**
	vas gipt es im **kee**noh?
Are there subtitles?	**Gibt es Untertitel?**
	gipt es **oon**ter-teetel?
When does the film start?	**Wann fängt der Film an?**
	van fengt dehr film an?
When does the film finish?	**Wann ist der Film zu Ende?**
	van ist dehr film tsoo **en**-de?
How much is it to get in?	**Was kostet der Eintritt?**
	vas **kos**tet dehr **yn**-trit?
Two for (name film)	**Zwei für...**
	tsvy fuer...

YOU MAY HEAR...

Für Kino 1/2...	For screen 1/2...
fuer **kee**noh yns/tsvy...	
ist ausverkauft	it's sold out
ist **ows**-ferkowft	

Theatre/opera

....

die Garderobe	cloakroom
dee gar-de-**roh**-be	
das Theaterstück	play
das teh-**ah**ter-shtuek	
der Platz dehr plats	seat

67

What's on at the theatre?	**Was gibt es im Theater?** vas gipt es im teh-**ah**ter?
How much are the tickets?	**Was kosten die Karten?** vas **kos**ten dee **kar**ten?
I'd like two tickets...	**Ich hätte gern zwei Karten...** ikh **het**-e gern tsvy **kar**ten...
for tonight	**für heute Abend** fuer **hoy**-te **ah**bent
in the stalls	**im Parkett** im par**ket**
in the circle	**im ersten Rang** im **er**sten rang
in the upper circle	**im zweiten Rang** im **tsvy**ten rang
When does the performance end?	**Wann ist die Vorstellung zu Ende?** van ist dee **fohr**-shtel<u>oo</u>ng tsoo **en**-de?

Television

die Fernbedienung dee **fern**-be**dee**noong	remote control
die Seifenoper dee **zy**fen-**oh**per	soap
der Videorecorder dehr **vee**deh-oh-re**kor**der	video recorder
die Nachrichten dee **nahkh**-rikhten	news
einschalten **yn**-shalten	to switch on
ausschalten **ows**-shalten	to switch off
der Cartoon dehr kar**toon**	cartoon

Is there a TV?
Gibt es hier einen Fernseher?
gipt es heer **yn**-en **fern**-zeh-er?

What's on television?
Was gibt es im Fernsehen?
vas gipt es im **fern**-zeh-en?

When is the news?
Wann kommen die Nachrichten?
van **kom**men **nahkh**-rikhten?

Please could you lower the volume?
Könnten Sie bitte leiser stellen?
kur'nten zee **bit**-e **ly**zer **shtell**en?

| May I turn the volume up? | **Darf ich lauter stellen?** |
| | darf ikh **low**ter **shtell**en? |

| Are there any English-language channels? | **Haben Sie englischsprachige Fernsehkanäle?** |
| | **hah**ben zee **eng**-lish-shprah-khi-ge **fern**-zeh-ka**neh**-le? |

| Do you have satellite TV? | **Haben Sie Satellitenfernsehen?** |
| | **hah**ben zee za-te-**lee**ten-**fern**-zeh-en? |

Sport

• •

der Wettkampf/das Spiel	match/game
dehr **vet**kampf/das shpeel	
der Tennisplatz	tennis court
dehr **tennis**-plats	
der Golfplatz	golf course
dehr **golf**-plats	
gewinnen ge-**vinn**en	to win

Where can we...?	**Wo können wir...?**
	voh **kur'**nen veer...?
play tennis	**Tennis spielen**
	tennis shpeelen

play golf	**Golf spielen**
	golf **shpee**len
go swimming	**schwimmen**
	shvimmen
go jogging	**joggen**
	joggen
go fishing	**angeln**
	ang-eln
go riding	**reiten**
	ryten
How much is it per hour?	**Was kostet es pro Stunde?**
	vas **kos**tet es proh **shtoon**-de?
Can we hire rackets/clubs?	**Kann man Schläger leihen?**
	kan man **shleh**ger **ly**-en?
Where can I/ we get tickets?	**Wo gibt es Karten?**
	voh gipt es **kar**ten?

Skiing

der Skipass dehr **shee**pas	ski pass
der Langlauf dehr **lang**lowf	cross-country skiing

I want to hire skis	**Ich möchte Skier leihen**
	ikh **mur'kh**-te **shee**-er **ly**-en
Are the boots/the poles included in the price?	**Sind die Schuhe/die Stöcke im Preis inbegriffen?**
	zint dee **shoo**-e/dee **shtur'**ke im prys **in**begriffen?
How much is a pass for...?	**Was kostet ein Pass für...?**
	vas **kos**tet yn pas fuer...?
a day	**einen Tag**
	yn-en tahk
a week	**eine Woche**
	yn-e **vokh**-e
Do you have a map of the ski runs?	**Haben Sie eine Pistenkarte?**
	hahben zee **yn**-e **pis**ten-kar-te?
When is the last chair-lift?	**Wann geht der letzte Skilift?**
	van geht dehr **let**-ste **shee**lift?

Es besteht Lawinengefahr es be**shteht** la-**vee**nen-ge**fahr**	There is danger of avalanches
Diese Piste ist gesperrt **dee**-ze **pis**-te ist ge**shpert**	This run is closed off

Walking

. . . .

Are there any guided walks?	**Gibt es geführte Wanderungen?** gipt es ge-**fuer**-te **van**der-roongen?
Is there a guide to local walks?	**Gibt es einen Wanderführer von dieser Gegend?** gipt es **yn**-en **van**der-**fuer**-rer fon **dee**zer **geh**gent?
How long is the walk?	**Wie lang ist die Wanderung?** vee lang ist dee **van**der-roong?
Is the path very steep?	**Ist der Weg sehr steil?** ist dehr vehg zehr shtyl?
How long will the walk take?	**Wie lange werden wir für die Wanderung brauchen?** vee **lang**-e **vehr**den veer fuer dee **van**der-roong **brow**-khen?

Walking

> **Maps and guides** (p 61)

73

Communications

Telephone and mobile

To phone Germany from the UK, dial the international code **oo 49**, then the German area code without the first o, e.g. Bonn (o)**228**, Leipzig (o)**341**, followed by the number you require. (Other international codes: Austria **oo 43**, Switzerland **oo 41**.) To phone the UK from Germany, dial **oo 44**, plus the UK area code without the first o, e.g. Glasgow (o)**141**. Most phone boxes take phonecards.

das Handy das **hen**dee	mobile
die Telefonkarte dee tele**fohn**-kar-te	phonecard
die Gelben Seiten dee gelben **zy**ten	Yellow Pages
das R-Gespräch das er-ge**shprehkh**	collect/reverse charge call

Kann ich mit Herrn.../Frau... sprechen?
kan ikh mit hern.../frow... **shprekh**-en?
Can I speak to Mr.../Mrs...?

Wer spricht, bitte?
ver shprikht **bit**-e?
Who is calling?

Hier ist Jim Brown
heer ist jim brown
This is Jim Brown

Besetzt. Soll ich etwas ausrichten?
be**zetst**. zoll ikh **et**vas **ows**-rikhten?
Engaged. Can I take a message?

Ich rufe später/morgen wieder an
ikh **roo**-fe **shpeh**ter/**mor**gen **vee**der an
I'll call back later/tomorrow

Where can I buy a phonecard?	**Wo kann ich eine Telefonkarte kaufen?** voh kan ikh **yn**-e tele**fohn**-kar-te **kow**fen?
A phonecard, please	**Eine Telefonkarte, bitte** **yn**-e tele**fohn**-kar-te **bit**-e
I want to make a phone call	**Ich möchte telefonieren** ikh **mur'kh**-te tele-fo-**neer**-ren
What is your mobile number?	**Wie lautet Ihre Handynummer?** vee **low**tet **eer**-re **hen**dee-**noomm**er?

75

My mobile number is...	**Meine Handynummer ist...**
	myn-e **hen**dee-**noomm**er ist...
Herr Braun, please	**Herrn Braun, bitte**
	hern brown, **bit**-e
Extension ..., please	**Apparat ..., bitte**
	apa-**raht** ..., **bit**-e
An outside line, please	**Eine Amtsleitung, bitte**
	yn-e **amts**-ly-<u>toong</u>, **bit**-e
I can't get through	**Ich komme nicht durch**
	ikh **kom**-e nikht <u>doorkh</u>
It's constantly engaged	**Da ist immer besetzt**
	da ist **imm**er be**zetst**

YOU MAY HEAR...

Augenblick, ich verbinde	Just a moment, I'm trying to connect you
owgen-blik, ikh fer**bin**-de	
Bitte rufen Sie später wieder an	Please try again later
bit-e **roo**fen zee **shpeh**ter **vee**der an	
Sie haben sich verwählt	You've got the wrong number
zee **hah**ben zikh fer**vehlt**	
Sie müssen Ihre Handys abschalten	You must turn off your mobile phones
zee **muess**en **eer**-re **hen**dees **ap**shalten	

Text messaging

• •

As is the case with many computer-related
expressions and indeed with everyday speech,
Germans tend to use a lot of English when writing
SMS. Most of the short forms used in mobile phone
messages are English abbreviations such as '4U'.

Can I text you? (informal)	**Kann ich dir eine SMS schicken?**
	kan ikh deer **yn**-e sms **shikk**en?
Can you text me? (informal)	**Kannst du mir eine SMS schicken?**
	kanst doo meer **yn**-e sms **shikk**en?
Good night!	**N8 (Gute Nacht!)**
Have a nice day!	**STN (SchönenTag noch!)**
(That was) cheeky!	**3st (Das war dreist)**
To be continued	**FF (Fortsetzung folgt)**
Attention! (Important!)	**8ung (Achtung)**
Phone me	**RUMIN (Ruf mich an)**
Shall we meet?	**TWU (Treffen wir uns?)**
I'll soon be there	**BIGBED (Bin gleich bei dir)**
I need money urgently	**BSG (Brauche sofort Geld)**
Miss you	**HASE (Habe Sehnsucht)**
Thinking of you	**DAD (Denk an dich)**
I feel so lonely	**BSE (Bin so einsam)**

I like you	MAD (Mag dich)
I love you	ILD (Ich liebe dich)
I'm happy	*freud* (Ich freue mich)
I'm sad	*heul* (Ich bin traurig)

E-mail

....

scannen	**skenn**en	to scan
drucken	**drookk**en	to print
CD-brennen		to burn CDs
tseh-**deh brenn**en		
downloaden		to download
downloaden		
löschen	**lur'sh**en	to delete

Do you have e-mail?	**Haben Sie E-Mail?** **hah**ben zee **ee**-mehl?
What's your e-mail address?	**Wie ist Ihre E-Mail-Adresse?** vee ist **eer**-re **ee**-mehl-a-**dres**-e?
How do you spell it?	**Wie buchstabiert man das?** vee **bookh**-shta-**beert** man das
All lower case	**Alles kleingeschrieben** **al**-es **klyn**-ge-shreeben
All upper case	**Alles großgeschrieben** **al**-es **grohs**-geshreeben
Can I send an e-mail?	**Kann ich eine E-Mail schicken?** kan ikh **yn**-e **ee**-mehl **shikk**en?

| Did you get my e-mail? | **Haben Sie meine E-Mail bekommen?** |
| | **hah**ben zee **myn**-e **ee**-mehl be**komm**en? |

Internet

•••••••••••••••••••••••••••••••••••••

German website addresses end in **.de** for **Deutschland** (Germany).

die Startseite	home
dee **shtart**-zy-te	
die Auswahl dee **ows**vahl	menu
der Benutzername	username
dehr be**noots**er-nah-me	
die Suchmaschine	search engine
dee **zookh**-mashee-ne	
das Passwort das **pas**vort	password

Are there any internet cafés here?	**Gibt es hier Internet-Cafés?**
	gipt es heer **in**ternet ka**fehs**?
How much is it to log on for an hour?	**Was kostet das Einloggen für eine Stunde?**
	vas **kos**tet das **yn**-loggen fuer **yn**-e **shtoon**de?
I can't log on	**Ich kann nicht einloggen**
	ikh kan nikht **yn**-loggen

Fax

Addressing a fax

an	to
von	from
Datum	date
Betreff:	re:
in der Anlage	please find attached
eine Kopie von...	a copy of...
...Seiten insgesamt	...pages in total

I want to send a fax	**Ich möchte ein Fax schicken** ikh **mur'kh**-te yn fax **shikk**en
Can I send a fax from here?	**Kann ich von hier ein Fax schicken?** kan ikh fon heer yn fax **shikk**en?
What is your fax number?	**Wie ist Ihre Faxnummer?** vee ist **eer**-re **fax**-n<u>oo</u>mmer?
My fax number is...	**Meine Faxnummer ist...** **myn**-e **fax**-n<u>oo</u>mmer ist...

Communications

Practicalities

Money

· ·

The euro is the currency of Germany. You can change money and travellers' cheques where you see the sign **Geldwechsel**. Cash dispensers usually let you choose which language to use for your transaction. Banks are generally open longer on Tuesdays and Thursdays.

Where can I change some money?	**Wo kann ich hier Geld wechseln?**
	voh kan ikh heer gelt **vek**seln?
Where is the nearest cash dispenser?	**Wo ist der nächste Geldautomat?**
	voh ist dehr **neh**-kste **gelt**-owtoh-**maht**?
When does the bank open?	**Wann macht die Bank auf?**
	van makht dee bank owf?
When does the bank close?	**Wann macht die Bank zu?**
	van makht dee bank tsoo?

I want to cash these travellers' cheques	**Ich würde gern diese Reiseschecks einlösen**	
	ikh **vuer**-de gern **dee**-ze **ry**-ze-sheks **yn**-lur'zen	
Can I use my credit card to get euros?	**Kann ich hier mit meiner Kreditkarte Euros bekommen?**	
	kan ikh heer mit **myn**-er kre**dit**-kar-te **oy**rohs be**komm**en?	

Paying

der Betrag dehr be**trahk**	amount to be paid	
die Rechnung dee **rekh**noong	bill	
die Kasse dee **kas**-e	cash desk	
die Quittung dee **kvitt**oong	receipt	

How much is it?	**Was kostet das?**	
	vas **kos**tet das?	
Can I pay...?	**Kann ich ... bezahlen?**	
	kan ikh ... be**tsah**len?	
by credit card	**mit Kreditkarte**	
	mit kre**dit**-kar-te	
by cheque	**mit Scheck**	
	mit shek	

Do you take credit cards?	**Nehmen Sie Kreditkarten?**
	nehmen zee kre**dit**-karten?
My credit card number is...	**Meine Kreditkartennummer ist...**
	myn-e kre**dit**-karten-**noomm**er ist...
expiry date...	**Auslaufdatum...**
	owslowf-**dah**toom...
valid until...	**Gültig bis...**
	gueltikh bis...
Is service/VAT included?	**Ist die Bedienung/die Mehrwertsteuer inbegriffen?**
	ist dee be-**dee**noong/dee **mehr**-vehrt-shtoyer **in**begriffen?
Put it on my bill	**Setzen Sie es auf meine Rechnung**
	zetsen zee es owf **myn**-e **rekh**noong
Could I have a receipt, please?	**Könnte ich eine Quittung haben, bitte?**
	kur'n-te ikh **yn**-e **kvitt**oong **hah**ben, **bit**-e?
Do I have to pay in advance?	**Muss ich im Voraus zahlen?**
	moos ikh im **fohr**-ows **tsah**len?
Do you require a deposit?	**Verlangen Sie eine Kaution?**
	fer**lang**en zee **yn**-e kow**tsiohn**?
Keep the change	**Stimmt so**
	shtimt zoh

> **Shopping** (p 53)

Luggage

You often need a coin to unlock the luggage trolley, so make sure you have some small change on arrival.

die Gepäckausgabe dee ge**pek-ows**-gah-be	baggage reclaim
die Gepäckaufbewahrung dee ge**pek-owf**-be-vahroong	left-luggage office
das Schliessfach das **shlees**fakh	left-luggage locker

My luggage isn't there	**Mein Gepäck ist nicht da** myn ge**pek** ist nikht dah
What's happened to the luggage on the flight from...?	**Was ist mit dem Gepäck vom Flug aus ... passiert?** vas ist mit dehm ge**pek** fom flook ows ... pa**seert**?
Can you help me with my luggage, please?	**Könnten Sie mir bitte mit meinem Gepäck helfen?** **kur'n**ten zee meer **bit**-e mit **myn**-em ge**pek hel**fen?

> **Train** (p 29) > **Air travel** (p 35)

Repairs

der Schuhmacher dehr **shoo**makher	shoe repair shop
die Schnellreparatur dee shnel-repara**toor**	repairs while you wait

This is broken	**Das ist kaputt** das ist ka**poot**
Where can I get this repaired?	**Wo kann ich das reparieren lassen?** voh kan ikh das repa**reer**-ren **lass**en?
Is it worth repairing?	**Lohnt sich die Reparatur?** lohnt zikh dee repara**toor**?
Can you repair...?	**Können Sie ... reparieren?** **kur**'nen zee ... repa**reer**-ren?
these shoes	**diese Schuhe** **dee**-ze **shoo**-e
my watch	**meine Uhr** **myn**-e oo-er

> **Breakdown** (p 42)

Complaints

. . . .

The ... doesn't/ don't work	**Der/Die/Das ... funktioniert nicht/Die ... funktionieren nicht**
	dehr/dee/das ... <u>foo</u>nk-tsio-**neert** nikht/dee ... <u>foo</u>nk-tsio-**neer**-ren nikht
light	**das Licht**
	das likht
lock	**das Schloss**
	das shlos
heating	**die Heizung**
	dee **hyt**<u>soo</u>ng
I want my money back	**Ich möchte mein Geld zurück**
	ikh **mur'kh**-te myn gelt tsoo**ruek**
This is dirty	**Das ist schmutzig**
	das ist **shmoot**sikh
We have been waiting for a very long time	**Wir warten schon sehr lange**
	veer **var**ten shohn zehr **lang**-e
The bill is not correct	**Die Rechnung stimmt nicht**
	dee **rekh**<u>noo</u>ng shtimt nikht

> **Hotel desk** (p 49)

Problems

....

Can you help me?	**Können Sie mir helfen?**
	kur'nen zee meer **hel**fen?
I don't speak German	**Ich spreche kein Deutsch**
	ikh **shprekh**-e kyn doytch
Does anyone here speak English?	**Spricht hier jemand Englisch?**
	shprikht heer **yeh**mant **eng**-lish?
What's the matter?	**Was ist los?**
	vas ist lohs?
I have a problem	**Ich habe ein Problem**
	ikh **hah**-be yn pro**blehm**
I'm lost (on foot)	**Ich habe mich verlaufen**
	ikh **hah**-be mikh fer**low**fen
How do I get to...?	**Wie komme ich nach...?**
	vee **kom**-e ikh nahkh...?
I've missed...	**Ich habe ... verpasst**
	ikh **hah**-be ... fer**past**
my plane	**mein Flugzeug**
	myn **flook**-tsoyk
my connection	**meinen Anschluss**
	myn-en **an**shloos
Can you show me how this works?	**Können Sie mir zeigen, wie das geht?**
	kur'nen zee meer **tsy**gen, vee das geht?
I've lost my money	**Ich habe mein Geld verloren**
	ikh **hah**-be myn gelt fer**loh**ren

Problems

87

I need to get to...	**Ich muss nach...**
	ikh m<u>oo</u>s nahkh...
Is there a lost property office?	**Gibt es hier ein Fundbüro?**
	gipt es heer yn **foont**-<u>bue</u>-roh?
Where is it?	**Wo ist es?**
	voh ist es?
Leave me alone!	**Lassen Sie mich in Ruhe!**
	lassen zee mikh in **roo**-e!
Go away!	**Hau ab!**
	how ap!

Emergencies

die Polizei dee poli**tsy**	police
der Krankenwagen dehr **krang**ken-**vah**gen	ambulance
die Feuerwehr dee **foy**er-vehr	fire brigade
die Notaufnahme dee **noht-owf**nah-me	casualty department

Help!	**Hilfe!**
	hil-fe!
Fire!	**Feuer!**
	foyer!
Can you help me?	**Können Sie mir helfen?**
	kur'nen zee meer **hel**fen?

Practicalities

There's been an accident	Ein Unfall ist passiert
	yn **oon**fal ist pa**seert**
Someone is injured	Es ist jemand verletzt worden
	es ist **yeh**mant fer**letzt vor**den
Someone has been run over	Es ist jemand überfahren worden
	es ist **yeh**mant ueber-**fah**ren **vor**den
Please call...	Bitte rufen Sie...
	bit-e **roo**fen zee...
the police	die Polizei
	dee poli**tsy**
an ambulance	einen Krankenwagen
	yn-en **krang**ken-**vah**gen
Where is the police station/ the hospital?	Wo ist die Polizeiwache/ das Krankenhaus?
	voh ist dee poli**tsy**-vakh-e/ das **krang**ken-hows?
I want to report a theft	Ich möchte einen Diebstahl melden
	ikh **mur'kh**-te **yn**-en **deep**-shtahl **mel**den
I've been robbed	Ich bin beraubt worden
	ikh bin be**rowpt vor**den
I've been attacked	Ich bin überfallen worden
	ikh bin ueber-**fall**en **vor**den
Someone has stolen...	Jemand hat ... gestohlen
	yehmant hat ... ge**shtoh**len

Emergencies

89

my money	**mein Geld**
	myn gelt
my passport	**meinen Pass**
	myn-en pas
My car has been broken into	**Mein Auto ist aufgebrochen worden**
	myn **owf**toh ist **owf**-gebrokh-en **vor**den
My car has been stolen	**Mein Auto ist gestohlen worden**
	myn **ow**toh ist ge**shtoh**len **vor**den
I've been raped	**Ich bin vergewaltigt worden**
	ikh bin fer-ge**val**tikt **vor**den
I want to speak to a policewoman	**Ich möchte mit einer Polizistin sprechen**
	ikh **mur'kh**-te mit **yn**-er poli**tsis**tin **shprekh**-en
I need to make an urgent telephone call	**Ich muss dringend telefonieren**
	ikh m<u>oo</u>s **dring**-ent tele-fo-**neer**-ren
I need a report for my insurance	**Ich brauche einen Bericht für meine Versicherung**
	ikh **brow**-khe **yn**-en be**rikht** fuer **myn**-e fer**zikh**er-r<u>oo</u>ng
How much is the fine?	**Wie viel Strafe muss ich zahlen?**
	vee feel **shtrah**-fe m<u>oo</u>s ikh **tsah**len

Where do I pay it?	**Wo kann ich das bezahlen?**
	voh kan ikh das be**tsah**len?
Do I have to pay it straightaway?	**Muss ich sofort bezahlen?**
	m<u>oo</u>s ikh zoh**fort** be**tsah**len?
I'm very sorry	**Es tut mir sehr leid**
	es toot meer zehr lyt
I would like to phone my embassy	**Ich möchte mit meiner Botschaft telefonieren**
	ikh **mur'kh**-te mit **myn**-er **boht**shaft telefo**neer**-ren

Sie sind bei Rot über die Ampel gefahren zee zint by roht **ueb**er dee **am**pel ge**fah**ren	You went through a red light
Sie sind zu schnell gefahren zee zint tsoo shnel ge**fah**ren	You were driving too fast

Emergencies

91

Health

Pharmacy

. . . .

die Apotheke dee apo-**teh**-ke	pharmacy
die Notapotheke dee **noht**-apo-**teh**-ke	duty chemist
das Rezept das re**tsept**	prescription

I don't feel well	**Ich fühle mich nicht wohl** ikh **fue**-le mikh nikht vohl
Have you something for...?	**Haben Sie etwas gegen...?** **hah**ben zee **et**vas **geh**gen...?
a headache	**Kopfschmerzen** **kopf**-shmertsen
car sickness	**Reisekrankheit** **ry**-ze-krank-hyt
diarrhoea	**Durchfall** **doorkh**fal
I have a rash	**Ich habe einen Ausschlag** ikh **hah**-be **yn**-en **ows**-shlahk

Dreimal täglich vor dem/ beim/nach dem Essen **dry**-mahl **tehk**likh fohr dehm/bym/nahkh dehm **ess**en	Three times a day before/with/after meals

Useful words

antiseptic	**das Antiseptikum**	anti-**zep**tik<u>oo</u>m
aspirin	**das Aspirin**	aspi-**reen**
cold	**die Erkältung**	er-**kelt**<u>oo</u>ng
condoms	**die Kondome**	kon**dohm**-e
cotton wool	**die Watte**	**vat**-e
dental floss	**die Zahnseide**	**tsahn**-zy-de
plaster	**das Pflaster**	**pflas**ter
sanitary pads	**die Binden**	**bin**den
sore throat	**die Halsschmerzen**	**hals**-shmertsen
tampons	**die Tampons**	**tam**pons
toothpaste	**die Zahnpasta**	**tsahn**-pasta

Pharmacy

93

Doctor

das Krankenhaus das **krang**ken-hows	hospital
die Ambulanz dee amboo**lants**	out-patients
die Sprechstunden dee **shprekh**-shtoonden	surgery hours

FACE TO FACE

A **Mein Sohn/Meine Tochter ist krank**
myn zohn/**myn**-e **tokh**ter ist krank
My son/My daughter is ill

B **Hat er/sie Fieber?**
hat ehr/zee **fee**ber?
Does he/she have a temperature?

A **Nein, er/sie hat Magenschmerzen**
nyn, ehr/zee hat **mah**gen-**shmer**tsen
No, he/she has a pain in the stomach

B **Er/Sie muss ins Krankenhaus**
ehr/zee moos ins **krang**ken-hows
He/She will have to go to hospital

I need a doctor	**Ich brauche einen Arzt** ikh **brow**-khe **yn**-en artst
I'm diabetic	**Ich habe Zucker** ikh **hah**-be **tsoo**ker

I'm pregnant	**Ich bin schwanger**
	ikh bin **shvang**-er
I'm on the pill	**Ich nehme die Pille**
	ikh **neh**-me dee **pil**-e
I'm allergic to penicillin	**Ich bin allergisch gegen Penizillin**
	ikh bin a-**ler**-gish **geh**gen peni-tsi**leen**
My blood group is...	**Meine Blutgruppe ist...**
	myn-e **bloot**groop-e ist...
Will I have to pay now?	**Muss ich gleich bezahlen?**
	moos ikh glykh be**tsah**len?
How much will it cost?	**Was wird es kosten?**
	vas virt es **kos**ten?
I need a receipt for the insurance	**Ich brauche eine Quittung für meine Versicherung**
	ikh **brow**-khe **yn**-e **kvitt**oong fuer **myn**-e fer**zikh**er-roong

YOU MAY HEAR...

Ich muss Sie röntgen ikh moos zee **rur'nt**gen	I'll have to do an X-ray

Dentist

die Füllung	filling
dee **fuell**oong	
die Krone dee **kroh**-ne	crown
die Prothese	dentures
dee pro-**teh**-ze	

I need a dentist	**Ich brauche einen Zahnarzt**
	ikh **brow**-khe yn-en **tsahn**artst
He/She has a toothache	**Er/Sie hat Zahnschmerzen**
	ehr/zee hat **tsahn**-shmertsen
Can you do a temporary filling?	**Können Sie mir eine provisorische Füllung machen?**
	kur'nen zee meer **yn**-e provi-**zoh**rish-e **fuell**oong **makh**en?
I think I have an abscess	**Ich glaube, ich habe einen Abszess**
	ikh **glow**-be, ikh **hah**-be yn-en aps-**tses**
It hurts	**Das tut weh**
	das toot veh
Can you give me something for the pain?	**Können Sie mir etwas gegen die Schmerzen geben?**
	kur'nen zee meer **et**vas **geh**gen dee **shmer**tsen **geh**ben?

Can you repair my dentures?	**Können Sie meine Prothese reparieren?**
	kur'nen zee **myn**-e pro-**teh**-ze repa-**reer**-ren?
Do I have to pay now?	**Muss ich das gleich bezahlen?**
	m<u>oo</u>s ikh das glykh be**tsah**len?
How much will it be?	**Wie teuer wird es?**
	vee **toy**er virt es?
I need a receipt for my insurance	**Ich brauche eine Quittung für meine Krankenkasse**
	ikh **brow**-khe **yn**-e **kvitt**<u>oo</u>ng fuer **myn**-e **krang**ken-kas-e

YOU MAY HEAR...

Bitte weit aufmachen **bit**-e vyt **owf**-makh-en	Please open wide
Möchten Sie eine Spritze? **mur'kh**ten zee **yn**-e **shprit**-se?	Do you want an injection?

Dentist

97

Different types of travellers

Disabled travellers

Do you have toilets for the disabled?	**Haben Sie Toiletten für Behinderte?** hahben zee twa-**lett**en fuer be-**hin**der-te?
Do you have any bedrooms on the ground floor?	**Haben Sie Zimmer im Erdgeschoss?** hahben zee **tsimm**er im **ert**-geshos?
How many steps are there?	**Wie viele Stufen sind es?** vee **fee**-le **shtoo**fen zint es?
Do you have a lift?	**Haben Sie einen Aufzug?** hahben zee **yn**-en **owf**tsook?
Where is the lift?	**Wo ist der Aufzug?** voh ist dehr **owf**tsook?
Do you have wheelchairs?	**Haben Sie Rollstühle?** hahben zee **rol**-shtue-le?

Is there an induction loop for the hard of hearing?	**Haben Sie eine Induktionsschleife für Schwerhörige?**
	hahben zee **yn**-e in-d<u>oo</u>k-**tsiohns**-shly-fe fuer **shvehr**-hur'-ri-ge?
Is there a reduction for the disabled?	**Gibt es eine Ermäßigung für Behinderte?**
	gipt es **yn**-e er-**meh**si-g<u>oo</u>ng fuer be-**hin**der-te?

With kids

. . . .

Public transport is free for children under 4.
Children between 4 and 12 pay half price.

A child's ticket	**Eine Kinderfahrkarte**
	yn-e **kin**der-**fahr**kar-te
He/She is ... years old	**Er/Sie ist ... Jahre alt**
	ehr/zee ist ... **yah**-re alt
Is there a reduction for children?	**Gibt es eine Ermäßigung für Kinder?**
	gipt es **yn**-e er-**meh**si-g<u>oo</u>ng fuer **kin**der?

With kids

> **Hotel (booking)** (p 47)

Do you have a children's menu?	**Haben Sie eine Speisekarte für Kinder?**
	hahben zee **yn**-e **shpy**-ze-kar-te fuer **kin**der?
Is it OK to take children?	**Kann man Kinder mitnehmen?**
	kan man **kin**der mit**neh**men?
Do you have...?	**Haben Sie...?**
	hahben zee...?
a high chair	**einen Hochstuhl**
	yn-en **hohkh**-shtool
a cot	**ein Kinderbett**
	yn **kin**derbet

> **Pharmacy** (p 92) > **Doctor** (p 94)

Reference

Alphabet

••••••••••••••••••••••••••••••••••••

Except for **ä**, **ö**, **ü** and **ß** (which corresponds to double **s**), the German alphabet is the same as the English. Below are the words used for clarification when spelling something out.

Wie schreibt man das? vee shrybt man das?	How do you spell it?
A wie Anton, B wie Berta ah vee **an**ton, beh vee **ber**ta	A for Anton, B for Berta

A (ä)	ah (ah **oom**lowt)	**Anton**	**an**ton
B	beh	**Berta**	**ber**ta
C	tseh	**Caesar**	**tseh**zahr
D	deh	**Dora**	**doh**rah
E	eh	**Emil**	**eh**meel
F	ef	**Friedrich**	**freed**rikh
G	geh	**Gustav**	**goos**taf
H	hah	**Heinrich**	**hyn**rikh
I	ee	**Ida**	**ee**dah

J	yot	**Julius**	**yoo**lee-<u>oo</u>s
K	kah	**Konrad**	**kon**raht
L	el	**Ludwig**	**lood**vikh
M	em	**Martin**	**mahr**tin
N	en	**Nordpol**	**nort**pohl
O (ö)	oh (oh **oom**lowt)	**Otto**	**ott**oh
P	peh	**Paula**	**pow**lah
Q	koo	**Quelle**	**kvell**-e
R	er	**Richard**	**rikh**art
S	es	**Siegfried**	**zeek**freet
ß	es-**tset**	**Eszett**	ess-**tset**
T	teh	**Theodor**	**teh**-o-dohr
U (ü)	oo (ue **oom**lowt)	**Ulrich**	**ool**rikh
V	fow	**Viktor**	**vik**tohr
W	veh	**Wilhelm**	**vil**helm
X	iks	**Xanten**	**ksan**ten
Y	**uep**silon	**Ypsilon**	**uep**silon
Z	tset	**Zeppelin**	**tse**-pe-leen

Measurements and quantities

• •

1 lb = approx. 0.5 kilo   1 pint = approx. 0.5 litre

Liquids

1/2 litre of... (c.1 pint)	**einen halben Liter...**
	yn-en **hal**ben **lee**ter
a litre of...	**einen Liter...**
	yn-en **lee**ter...
a bottle of...	**eine Flasche...**
	yn-e **flash**-e...
a glass of...	**ein Glas...**
	yn glahs...
a small glass	**ein kleines Glas**
	yn **klyn**-es glahs
a large glass	**ein großes Glas**
	yn **groh**-ses glahs

Weights

100 grams of...	**hundert Gramm...**
	hoondert gram...
a pound (=500 g)	**ein Pfund**
	yn pf<u>oo</u>nt

103

| a kilo of... | **ein Kilo...** |
| | yn **kee**loh... |

Food

a slice of...	**eine Scheibe...**
	yn-e **shy**-be...
a portion of...	**eine Portion...**
	yn-e por-**tsiohn**...
a dozen...	**ein Dutzend...**
	yn **doot**sent...
a packet of...	**ein Paket...**
	yn pa**keht**...
a tin of...	**eine Dose...**
	yn-e **doh**-ze...
a jar of...	**ein Glas...**
	yn glahs...

Miscellaneous

10 euros worth of...	**für zehn Euro...**
	fuer tsehn **oy**roh...
a third	**ein Drittel**
	yn **dritt**el
a quarter	**ein Viertel**
	yn **feer**tel
ten per cent	**zehn Prozent**
	tsehn pro**tsent**

more...	**noch etwas...**
	nokh **et**vas...
less...	**weniger...**
	vehni-ger...
enough	**genug**
	ge**nook**
double	**doppelt**
	doppelt
twice	**zweimal**
	tsvymahl
three times	**dreimal**
	drymahl

Numbers

. . . .

0	**null** <u>nool</u>
1	**eins** yns
2	**zwei** tsvy
3	**drei** dry
4	**vier** feer
5	**fünf** <u>fuenf</u>
6	**sechs** zeks
7	**sieben zee**ben
8	**acht** akht
9	**neun** noyn
10	**zehn** tsehn

11	**elf** elf
12	**zwölf** tsv<u>ur</u>'lf
13	**dreizehn dry**-tsehn
14	**vierzehn feer**-tsehn
15	**fünfzehn fuenf**-tsehn
16	**sechzehn zekh**-tsehn
17	**siebzehn zeep**-tsehn
18	**achtzehn akh**-tsehn
19	**neunzehn noyn**-tsehn
20	**zwanzig tsvan**-tsikh
21	**einundzwanzig yn**-<u>oo</u>nt-tsvan-tsikh
22	**zweiundzwanzig tsvy**-<u>oo</u>nt-tsvan-tsikh
23	**dreiundzwanzig dry**-<u>oo</u>nt-tsvan-tsikh
24	**vierundzwanzig feer**-<u>oo</u>nt-tsvan-tsikh
25	**fünfundzwanzig fuenf**-<u>oo</u>nt-tsvan-tsikh
30	**dreißig dry**-sikh
40	**vierzig feer**-tsikh
50	**fünfzig fuenf**-tsikh
60	**sechzig zekh**-tsikh
70	**siebzig zeep**-tsikh
80	**achtzig akh**-tsikh
90	**neunzig noyn**-tsikh
100	**hundert hoon**dert
101	**hunderteins hoon**dert-yns
200	**zweihundert tsvy**-h<u>oo</u>ndert
1,000	**tausend tow**zent
2,000	**zweitausend tsvy**-towzent
1 million	**eine Million yn**-e mil**iohn**

1st	**erste ehrs**-te
2nd	**zweite tsvy**-te
3rd	**dritte drit**-e
4th	**vierte feer**-te
5th	**fünfte fuenf**-te
6th	**sechste zeks**-te
7th	**siebte zeep**-te
8th	**achte akh**-te
9th	**neunte noyn**-te
10th	**zehnte tsehn**-te

Days and months

Days (all **der** words)

Monday	**Montag**	**mohn**-tahk
Tuesday	**Dienstag**	**deens**-tahk
Wednesday	**Mittwoch**	**mit**-vokh
Thursday	**Donnerstag**	**donn**ers-tahk
Friday	**Freitag**	**fry**-tahk
Saturday	**Samstag**	**zams**-tahk
Sunday	**Sonntag**	**zon**-tahk

Months (all **der** words)

January	**Januar**	**yan<u>oo</u>**-ahr
February	**Februar**	**fehb**r<u>oo</u>-ahr
March	**März**	merts
April	**April**	ap**ril**
May	**Mai**	my
June	**Juni**	**yoo**nee
July	**Juli**	**yoo**lee
August	**August**	ow**goost**
September	**September**	zep**tem**ber
October	**Oktober**	ok**toh**ber
November	**November**	no**vem**ber
December	**Dezember**	deh**tsem**ber

Seasons (all **der** words)

spring	**Frühling**	**frue**ling
summer	**Sommer**	**zomm**er
autumn	**Herbst**	herpst
winter	**Winter**	**vin**ter

| What is today's date? | **Was für ein Datum haben wir heute?** |
| | was fuer yn **dah**<u>toom</u> **hah**ben veer **hoy**-te? |

It's the 5th of March 2003	**Heute ist der fünfte März zweitausenddrei**
	hoy-te ist dehr **fuenf**-te merts **tsvy**-towzent-**dry**
on Saturday	**am Samstag**
	am **zams**-tahk
on Saturdays	**samstags**
	zams-tahks
every Saturday	**jeden Samstag**
	yehden **zams**-tahk
this Saturday	**diesen Samstag**
	deezen **zams**-tahk
next Saturday	**nächsten Samstag**
	neh-ksten **zams**-tahk
last Saturday	**letzten Samstag**
	letsten **zams**-tahk
in June	**im Juni**
	im **yoo**nee
at the beginning of June	**Anfang Juni**
	anfang **yoo**nee
at the end of June	**Ende Juni**
	en-de **yoo**nee
before the summer	**vor dem Sommer**
	fohr dehm **zomm**er
during the summer	**im Sommer**
	im **zomm**er
after the summer	**nach dem Sommer**
	nahkh dehm **zomm**er

Time

....

The 24-hour clock is used a lot more in continental
Europe than in Britain. After 12.00 midday, it continues:
13.00 - dreizehn Uhr, **14.00 - vierzehn Uhr**,
15.00 - fünfzehn Uhr, etc. until **24.00 -
vierundzwanzig Uhr**. With the 24-hour clock, the
words **viertel** (quarter) and **halb** (half) aren't used:

13.15 (1.15pm)	**dreizehn Uhr fünfzehn**
19.30 (7.30pm)	**neunzehn Uhr dreißig**
22.45 (10.45pm)	**zweiundzwanzig Uhr fünfundvierzig**
What time is it, please?	**Wie spät ist es, bitte?**
	vee shpeht ist es, **bit**-e?
am	**morgens**
	morgens
pm	**abends**
	ahbents
It's ...	**Es ist...**
	es ist...
2 o'clock	**zwei Uhr**
	tsvy oo-er
3 o'clock	**drei Uhr**
	dry oo-er
6 o'clock (etc.)	**sechs Uhr**
	zeks oo-er

It's half past 8	**Es ist halb neun** (in German you say half to 9)
	es ist halp noyn
at midnight	**um Mitternacht**
	<u>oo</u>m **mitt**er-nakht
9	**neun Uhr**
	noyn oo-er
9.10	**neun Uhr zehn**
	noyn oo-er tsehn
quarter past 9	**Viertel nach neun** (Austria: **viertel zehn**)
	feertel nahkh noyn
9.20	**neun Uhr zwanzig**
	noyn oo-er **tswan**-tsikh
half past 9/9.30	**halb zehn/neun Uhr dreißig**
	halp tsehn/noyn oo-er **dry**-sikh
9.35	**neun Uhr fünfunddreißig**
	noyn oo-er **fuenf**-<u>oo</u>nt-**dry**-sikh
quarter to 10	**Viertel vor zehn** (Austria: **drei viertel zehn**)
	feertel fohr tsehn
10 to 10	**zehn vor zehn**
	tsehn fohr tsehn

Time phrases

....

When do you open?	**Wann öffnen Sie?**
	van **ur'f**nen zee?
When do you close?	**Wann schließen Sie?**
	van **shlee**-sen zee?
at 3 o'clock	**um drei Uhr**
	<u>oo</u>m dry oo-er
before 3 o'clock	**vor drei Uhr**
	fohr dry oo-er
after 3 o'clock	**nach drei Uhr**
	nahkh dry oo-er
today	**heute**
	hoy-te
tonight	**heute Abend**
	hoy-te **ah**bent
tomorrow	**morgen**
	morgen
yesterday	**gestern**
	gestern

Eating out

Eating places

• •

Café Sometimes attached to a cake shop, **Konditorei**, where you can sit down and sample some of the cakes. Can be quite expensive.

Biergarten An open-air pub offering a selection of meals, usually hearty food (like soups or sausages).

Selbstbedienung Self-service.

Bistro A good place for breakfast, snacks, coffees and cakes.

Eisdiele/Eiscafé Ice-cream parlour.

In a bar/café

FACE TO FACE

A **Was möchten Sie?**
vas **mur'kh**ten zee?
What can I get you?

B **Wir möchten einen schwarzen Kaffee/**
Milchkaffee und einen Tee mit Milch/
Zitrone/ohne Zucker
veer **mur'kh**ten **yn**-en **shvar**-tsen ka**feh**/
milkh-kafeh <u>oo</u>nt **yn**-en teh mit milkh/tsi**troh**-ne/
oh-ne **tsoo**ker
We would like a black/white coffee and a tea with
milk/lemon/no sugar

A **Darf es sonst noch etwas sein?**
darf es zonst nokh **et**vas zyn?
Would you like anything else?

B **Das ist alles, danke**
das ist **al**-es, **dang**-ke
That's all, thank you

I'd like something cool to drink	**Ich möchte etwas Kühles trinken** ikh **mur'kh**-te **et**vas **kue**les **tring**ken

Do you have anything non-alcoholic?	**Haben Sie auch Getränke ohne Alkohol?**
	hahben zee owkh ge-**treng**-ke **oh**-ne **al**ko-hohl?
a bottle of mineral water	**eine Flasche Mineralwasser**
	yn-e **flash**-e mi-ne-**rahl**-vasser
sparkling	**mit Kohlensäure**
	mit **kohl**en-zoy-re
still	**still**
	shtill
for two	**für zwei**
	fuer tsvy
for me	**für mich**
	fuer mikh
for him/her	**für ihn/sie**
	fuer een/zee
for us	**für uns**
	fuer <u>oo</u>ns
with ice	**mit Eis**
	mit ys
a lager	**ein helles Bier**
	yn **hel**-es beer
a bitter	**ein Altbier**
	yn **alt**beer
a half pint	**ein Kleines**
	yn **klyn**-es
a pint (approx.)	**ein Großes**
	yn **groh**-ses

Other drinks to try

ein Kölsch a strong lager from Cologne
ein dunkles Bier a dark beer similar to brown ale
einen Fruchtsaft a fruit juice
eine heiße Schokolade a rich-tasting hot chocolate
ein Pils a strong, slightly bitter lager
einen Radler a type of shandy

Reading the menu

Typical German snack food (**Imbiss**) includes
Bratwurst (fried sausage), **Bockwurst** (boiled sausage, e.g. frankfurter) and **Buletten** (thick hamburgers).

Getränke nicht inklusive drinks not included

Tagesgericht für 7,50 € dish of the day €7.50

Mittagsmenü lunchtime menu

Vorspeise + Hauptgericht + Kaffee starter + main course + coffee

Speisekarte	menu
Vorspeisen	starters
Suppen	soups
Salate	salads
Knoblauchbrot	garlic bread
Fleisch	meat
Wild und Geflügel	game & poultry
Fisch	fish
Meeresfrüchte	seafood
Gemüse	vegetables
Käse	cheese
Dessert	dessert
Getränke	drinks

In a restaurant

In Germany the main meal of the day is lunch –
Mittagessen. Breakfast – **Frühstück** – is also often
a substantial meal. Look out for breakfast buffets –
Frühstücksbüfett.

A **Ich möchte einen Tisch für heute Abend/
morgen Abend/acht Uhr reservieren**
ikh **mur'kh**-te **yn**-en tish fuer **hoy**-te **ah**bent/**mor**gen
ahbent/akht oo-er re-zer-**veer**-ren
I'd like to book a table for tonight/tomorrow night/
8 pm

B **Für wie viele Personen?**
fuer vee **fee**-le per-**zoh**nen?
For how many people?

The menu, please	**Die Speisekarte, bitte**
	dee **shpy**-ze-kar-te, **bit**-e
What is the dish of the day?	**Was ist das Tagesgericht?**
	vas ist das **tah**ges-ge-**rikht**?
Have you a set-price menu?	**Haben Sie eine Tageskarte?**
	hahben zee **yn**-e **tah**ges-kar-te?
I'll have this	**Ich nehme das**
	ikh **neh**-me das
What is in this?	**Was ist das?**
	vas ist das?
Can you recommend a local dish?	**Können Sie eine Spezialität aus der Gegend empfehlen?**
	kur'nen zee **yn**-e shpetsi-ali-**teht** ows dehr **geh**gent emp-**feh**len?
Excuse me!	**Entschuldigung!**
	ent**shool**di-goong!

more bread...	**noch etwas Brot...**
	nokh **et**vas broht...
more water...	**noch etwas Wasser...**
	nokh **et**vas **vass**er...
please	**bitte**
	bit-e
The bill, please	**Zahlen, bitte**
	tsahlen, **bit**-e
Is service included?	**Ist die Bedienung inbegriffen?**
	ist dee be-**dee**n<u>oo</u>ng **in**begriffen?

Vegetarian

Although vegetarianism is slowly becoming more popular, few restaurants offer vegetarian options.

Are there any vegetarian restaurants here?	**Gibt es hier vegetarische Restaurants?**
	gipt es heer ve-ge-**tah**rish-e restoh-**rants**?
Do you have any vegetarian dishes?	**Haben Sie vegetarische Gerichte?**
	hahben zee ve-ge-**tah**rish-e ge-**rikh**-te?
Which dishes have no meat/fish?	**Welche Gerichte sind ohne Fleisch/Fisch?**
	vel-khe ge-**rikh**-te zint **oh**-ne flysh/fish?

119

What fish dishes do you have?	**Was für Fischgerichte haben Sie?**
	vas fuer **fish**-ge-rikh-te **hah**ben zee?
I'd like pasta as a main course	**Ich möchte als Hauptgericht Nudeln**
	ikh **mur'kh**-te als **howpt**-ge-rikht **noo**deln
I don't eat meat	**Ich esse kein Fleisch**
	ikh **es**-e kyn flysh
What do you recommend?	**Was können Sie empfehlen?**
	vas **kur'**nen zee emp**feh**len?
Is it made with vegetable stock?	**Ist das mit Gemüsebrühe gemacht?**
	ist das mit ge**mue**-ze-**brue**-e ge-**makht**?

Possible dishes

Gemüsestrudel vegetable strudel
Kartoffelpuffer potato pancakes
Käseplatte cheese platter
Omelette mit Champignons mushroom omelette
Pfifferlinge mit Semmelklops chanterelle mushrooms with dumpling and sauce
Topfenstrudel strudel filled with soft cheese

Wines and spirits

The wine list, please	**Die Weinkarte, bitte**
	dee **vyn**kar-te, **bit**-e
Can you recommend a good wine?	**Können Sie mir einen guten Wein empfehlen?**
	kur'nen zee meer **yn**-en **goo**ten vyn emp**feh**len?
a bottle of house wine	**eine Flasche Hauswein**
	yn-e **flash**-e **hows**vyn
a glass of white wine/red wine	**ein Glas Weißwein/Rotwein**
	yn glahs **vys**vyn/**roht**vyn
a bottle of red wine	**eine Flasche Rotwein**
	yn-e **flash**-e **roht**vyn
a bottle of white wine	**eine Flasche Weißwein**
	yn-e **flash**-e **vys**vyn

Wines

Wines are usually categorized according to three criteria: the growing area, the village or even vineyard where they are produced, and the type of grape they are made from. Major grape varieties include **Riesling**, **Silvaner**, **Gewürztraminer** and **Müller-Thurgau**.

Important wine-growing areas in Germany and Austria include:

Ahr small valley north of the Moselle, producing mainly light red wines

Baden the region around Freiburg in the Upper Rhine valley, producing light, mainly white and rosé wines

Burgenland region in Austria, producing mainly sweet wines

Franken important wine-growing area in Northern Bavaria,producing dry, full-bodied wines

Mosel-Saar-Ruwer region along the rivers Moselle, Saar and Ruwer, producing white wines, many of them dry

Rheinpfalz Palatinate region, producing mainly white wines

Rheinhessen quality wine region along the banks of the Rhine

Wachau major wine-growing area in Austria, just west of Vienna

The wine-producing villages and vineyards are innumerable. The name of the wine often consists of the name of the village (e.g. **Nierstein**) followed by the name of the particular vineyard (e.g. **Gutes Domtal**), which combined becomes **Niersteiner Gutes Domtal**.

Other words to look out for are:

Eiswein a rich, naturally sweet, white wine made from grapes that are harvested after a period of frost
halbtrocken medium-dry
Landwein wine of similar quality to French 'vin de pays'
lieblich sweet
Prädikatswein highest category of quality wines
QbA good-quality wine from a specified region
Tafelwein lowest-quality wine, similar to French 'vin de table'
trocken dry

Other drinks

What liqueurs do you have?	**Was für Liköre haben Sie?**
	vas fuer li-**kur'**-re **hah**ben zee?

Apfelkorn apple brandy
Danziger Goldwasser brandy with tiny bits of gold leaf
Himbeergeist strong, clear raspberry brandy
Kirschwasser cherry brandy
Schnaps strong spirit
Sliwowitz plum brandy (Austria)

Wines and spirits

Menu reader

Aal eel
　Aalsuppe eel soup
Allgäuer Emmentaler whole-milk hard cheese from the Allgäu
Allgäuer Käsespätzle cheese noodles from the Allgäu
Alpzirler cow's milk cheese from Austria
Alsterwasser lager shandy
Altbier top-fermented beer from the Lower Rhine
Ananas pineapple
Apfel apple
Apfelkorn apple brandy
　Apfelkuchen apple cake
　Apfelmus apple puree
　Apfelsaft apple juice
　Apfelsalami salami with apple
　Apfelstrudel flaky pastry filled with apples and spices
　Apfelwein cider (apple wine)
Aprikose apricot
Arme Ritter French toast
Art style or mode of preparation, e.g. **nach Art des Hauses** = à la maison

Artischocken artichokes
Aubergine aubergine
Auflauf baked dish, can be sweet or savoury
Aufschnitt sliced cold meats
Austern oysters

Bäckerofen 'baker's oven', pork and lamb bake
  from the Saarland region
Backpflaumen prunes
Banane banana
Bandnudeln ribbon pasta
Barack apricot brandy
Barsch perch
Bauernfrühstück cooked breakfast of scrambled
  eggs, bacon, diced potatoes, onions, tomatoes
Baunzerl little bread roll with distinctive cut on top
  (Austria)
Bayrisch Kraut shredded cabbage cooked with
  sliced apples, wine and sugar
Beilage side dish
Bereich Bernkastel area along the Moselle,
  producing crisp white wines
Bergkäse cheese from the Alps
Berliner doughnut filled with jam
Berliner Weiße fizzy beer with fruit syrup added
Berner Erbsensuppe soup made of dried peas
  with pig's trotters
Bienenstich type of cake, baked on a tray with a
  coating of almonds and sugar and a cream filling

Bierschinken ham sausage
Bierteig pastry made with beer
Bierwurst Bavarian boiled sausage
Birchermüsli muesli with yoghurt (Switzerland)
Birne pear
  Birnen, Bohnen und Speck (Northern Germany)
  pears, green beans and bacon
  Birne Helene dessert with vanilla ice cream, pear,
  and chocolate sauce
  Birnenmost pear wine
  Birnensekt sparkling pear wine
Blätterteig puff pastry
Blätterteigpastete vol-au-vent
Blattsalat green salad
blau rare (meat); poached (fish)
Blauschimmelkäse blue cheese
Blumenkohl cauliflower
Blunz'n black pudding (South Germany and Austria)
Blutwurst black pudding
Bockbier strong beer (light or dark), drunk
  especially in Bavaria
Bockwurst boiled sausage. A popular snack served
  with a bread roll
Böhmische Knödel sliced dumpling
Bohnen beans
  Bohnensuppe thick bean and bacon soup
Bosniakerl wholemeal roll with caraway seeds
Brathähnchen roast chicken
Brathering fried herring (eaten cold)

Bratkartoffeln fried potatoes

Bratwurst fried sausage. A popular snack served with a bread roll

Brauner strong black coffee with a little milk

Bremer Kükenragout Bremen chicken fricassée

Brezel (or in Bavaria: **Brezn**) pretzel

Broiler spit-roasted chicken (East German)

Brombeeren blackberries

Bröselknödel soup with little dumplings prepared with bone marrow and breadcrumbs

Brot bread

Brötchen bread roll

Brühe clear soup

Brühwurst thick frankfurter

B'soffene pudding soaked in mulled wine

Buletten thick hamburgers (but without the bread)

  Buletten mit Kartoffelsalat thick hamburgers with potato salad

Bündnerfleisch raw beef, smoked and dried, served thinly sliced

Burgenländische Krautsuppe thick cabbage and vegetable soup

Butter butter

  Butterbrot open sandwich

  Butterkäse high-fat cheese

Cervelat fine beef and pork salami

Chindbettering ring of bread

Cremeschnitten cream slices

Champagner champagne

Champignons button mushrooms

Cordon bleu veal escalope filled with boiled ham and cheese, covered in breadcrumbs

Currywurst sausage served with a spicy sauce. A popular snack originally from Berlin

Damenkäse mild buttery cheese

Dampfnudeln hot yeast dumplings

Datteln dates

Deutsches Beefsteak thick hamburger (but without the bread)

dicke Bohnen broad beans

Doppelbockbier like **Bockbier**, but even stronger

Dorsch cod

Dresdner Suppentopf Dresden vegetable soup with dumplings (East German)

Dunkles dark beer

Ei egg

  Eier im Glas soft-boiled eggs, served in a glass

Eierkuchen pancakes

Eierschwammerln chanterelles

Eierspeispfandl special Viennese omelette

eingelegt pickled

Einmachsuppe chicken or veal broth with cream and egg

Einspänner coffee with whipped cream, served in a glass (Austria)

Eintopf stew

Eis ice cream

Eisbecher knickerbocker glory

Eisbein boiled pork knuckle, often served with sauerkraut

Eiskaffee iced coffee, served with vanilla ice cream

Eiswein a rich, naturally sweet, white wine made from grapes harvested after a period of frost

Emmentaler whole-milk hard cheese

Ennstaler blue cheese from mixed milk

Ente duck

Erbach area producing scented white wines, mainly from the Riesling grape

Erbsen peas

  Erbsenpüree green pea purée

  Erbsensuppe pea soup

Erdäpfel potatoes (Austria)

  Erdäpfelgulasch spicy sausage and potato stew

  Erdäpfelknödel potato and semolina dumplings

  Erdäpfelkren relish with potato and horseradish (Austria)

  Erdäpfelnudeln fried balls of boiled potato, tossed in fried breadcrumbs

Erdbeeren strawberries

Erdnüsse peanuts

erster Gang first course

Essig vinegar

Export-Bier premium beer

Falscher Hase baked mince meatloaf

Fasan pheasant

Feigen figs

Fenchel fennel

fettarm low in fat

Fisch fish

  Fischgerichte fish and seafood dishes

  Fischklöße fish dumplings

  Fischsuppe fish soup

flambiert flambé

Fledermaus boiled beef in horseradish cream

Fleisch meat

  Fleischgerichte meat dishes

  Fleischklößchen meatballs

  Fleischlaberln highly seasoned meat cake (Austria)

  Fleischpflanzerl thick hamburgers

  Fleischsalat sausage salad with onions

  Fleischsuppe meat soup served with dumplings

Flunder flounder

Fondue melted cheese with wine and bread for dipping

Forelle trout

  Forelle blau steamed trout with potatoes and vegetables

  Forelle Müllerin trout fried in batter with almonds

  Forelle Steiermark trout fillet with bacon in white sauce

Frikadelle meatball, rissole

frisch fresh

Fritattensuppe beef broth with strips of pancake (Austria)

frittiert fried

Froschschenkel frogs' legs

Frucht fresh fruit

Früchtetee fruit tea

Fruchtsaft fruit juice

Fünfkernbrot wholemeal bread made with five different cereals

Gang course

Gans goose

  Gänseleber foie gras

  Gänseleberpastete goose liver pâté

Gebäck pastries

gebacken baked

gebackene Leber liver fried in breadcrumbs

gebraten roasted/fried

gedämpft steamed

Geflügel poultry

gefüllt stuffed/filled

  gefüllte Kalbsbrust stuffed breast of veal

  gefüllte Paprika peppers filled with mince

gegrillt grilled

  gegrillter Lachs grilled salmon

Gehacktes mince

gekocht boiled

  gekochtes Rindfleisch mit grüner Soße boiled beef with green sauce

gemischter Salat mixed salad

Gemüse vegetables

  Gemüse und Klöße vegetables and dumplings

  Gemüselasagne vegetable lasagne

  Gemüseplatte mixed vegetables

  Gemüsesuppe vegetable soup

geräuchert smoked

Gericht dish

geschmort braised

Geschnetzeltes thinly sliced meat in sauce, served with potatoes or rice

Geselchtes smoked meats (Austria)

Gespritzter spritzer, white wine and soda water

Gewürzgurken gherkins

Gitziprägel baked rabbit in batter (a Swiss dish)

Glühwein mulled wine

Goldbarsch redfish

Graf Görz Austrian soft cheese

Grammeln croissant stuffed with bacon

Grießklößchensuppe soup with semolina dumplings

Grießtaler gnocchi

Grog hot rum

grüne Bohnen green beans

grüne Veltlinersuppe green wine soup

grüner Salat green salad

Grünkohl kale

Gruyère gruyère cheese

Güggeli roast chicken with onions and mushrooms in white wine sauce (Switzerland)

Gulasch stewed diced beef or pork with paprika
Gulaschsuppe spicy meat soup with paprika
Gulyas beef stew with paprika
Gumpoldskirchner spicy white wine from Austria
Gurke cucumber
 Gurkensalat cucumber salad
gutbürgerliche Küche traditional German cooking
Gyros donner kebab

Hackbraten mincemeat roast
Hackepeter auf Schrippen mit Zwiebeln spiced
 minced pork on rolls, with onions
Hackfleisch mince
Hähnchen chicken
 Hähnchenbrust chicken breast
halbtrocken medium-dry
Hamburger Rundstück Hamburg meat roll
Hammel mutton
Hartkäse hard cheese
Hase hare
Hasenbraten roast hare
Hasenpfeffer rabbit stew
Hauptgericht main course
Hausbrauerei house brewery
hausgemacht home-made
Hausmannskost good traditional home cooking
Hawaiitoast toast with cooked ham, pineapple
 slice and melted cheese
Hecht pike

Hefeweizen wheat beer
Heidschnuckenragout lamb stew
heiß hot
Helles light beer
Hering herring
  Heringsschmaus herring in creamy sauce
Herz heart
Heuriger new wine
Himbeeren raspberries
  Himbeergeist raspberry brandy
Hirn brain
Hirsch venison
Hockheim strong white wines from the Rheingau
Honig honey
Hühnchen chicken
Hühnerfrikasse chicken fricassée
Hühnerschenkel chicken drumsticks
Hühnerleber chicken liver
Hummer lobster

Ingwer ginger

Jägerschnitzel escalope served with mushrooms
  and wine sauce
Jogurt yoghurt
Johannisbeeren currants (red, black or white)
Jura-Omelette bacon, potato and onion omelette

Kabeljau cod
Kaffee coffee
  Kaffee komplett coffee with milk and sugar
  Kaffee mit Milch coffee with milk
  koffeinfreier Kaffee decaf
Kaisermelange black coffee with an egg yolk
Kaiserschmarren strips of pancake served with raisins, sugar and cinnamon
Kakao cocoa
Kalb veal
  Kalbsbraten roast veal
  Kalbshaxe knuckle of veal
  Kalbskotelett veal escalope
  Kalbsleber calf's liver
  Kalbsschnitzel veal escalope
kalt cold
  kalte Platte cold meat platter
Kaninchen rabbit
Kapuziner Austrian equivalent to a cappuccino, which is black coffee with a drop of milk
Karotten carrots
Karpfen carp
  Karpfen blau poached carp
  Karpfen in Bier carp poached in beer with herbs
Kartoffeln potatoes
  Kartoffelklöße potato dumplings
  Kartoffelpuffer potato pancakes. A popular snack

Kartoffelpüree mashed potatoes
Kartoffelsalat potato salad
Kartoffelsuppe potato soup
Käse cheese
Käsebrötchen roll with small bacon pieces in the dough and melted cheese on top
Käsefondue dish made from melted cheese with wine and kirsch, into which you dip bread
Käsekuchen cheesecake
Käsenudeln noodles served with cheese
Käseplatte cheese platter
Käsesuppe cheese soup
Kasseler smoked pork
Kasseler Rippe mit Sauerkraut smoked pork rib with sauerkraut
Kastanienroulade roulade with chestnut filling
Katenspeck streaky bacon
Kaviar caviar
Kekse biscuits
Kirschen cherries
Kirschwasser cherry brandy
Kirtagssuppe soup with caraway seeds, thickened with potato (Austria)
Klops rissole
Klöße dumplings
Knackwurst hot spicy sausage, a popular snack served with bread
Knoblauch garlic

Knödel dumpling
  Knödelbeignets fruit dumplings
Knöderl dumplings (Austria)
Kohl cabbage
Kohlrouladen stuffed cabbage
Kohlsprossen Brussels sprouts
Kölsch top-fermented beer from Cologne
Kompott stewed fruit
Konfitüre jam
Königsberger Klopse meatballs served in thick
  white sauce with capers
Kopfsalat lettuce salad
Korn rye spirit
Kotelett pork chop/escalope dipped in
  breadcrumbs and deep fried
Krabben prawns
  Krabbencocktail prawn cocktail
Kraftbrot wheatgerm bread
Kraftfleisch corned beef
Kraftsuppe consommé
Krapfen doughnut
Kräuter herbs
Kräutertee herbal tea
Krautwicke(r)l stuffed cabbage
Krebs crawfish, crab
Kren horseradish
Kristallweizen a type of sparkling beer
Kroketten croquettes

Kuchen cake
Kürbis pumpkin

Labskaus cured pork, herring and potato stew
Lachs salmon
  Lachsbrot smoked salmon with bread
Lamm lamb
Lammkeule leg of lamb
Languste spiny lobster
Lasagne lasagne
Lauch leeks
Leber liver
Leberkäse pork liver meatloaf
Leberknödelsuppe light soup with chicken liver
  dumplings
Leberpastete liver paté
Leberwurst liver sausage
Lebkuchen gingerbread
Leinsamenbrot wholemeal bread with linseed
Leipziger Allerlei vegetable dish made from peas,
  carrots, cauliflower and cabbage (East German)
Lendenbraten roast loin
lieblich sweet (wine)
Likör liqueur
Limburger strong cheese flavoured with herbs
Limonade lemonade
Linsen lentils
  Linsen-Speck-Salat lentil salad with bacon
  Linsensuppe lentil and sausage soup

Linzer Torte latticed tart with jam topping
Liptauer Quark cream cheese with paprika and herbs
Lunge lungs

Mais sweetcorn
Maiskolben corn on the cob
Makrele mackerel
Malzbier dark malt beer
Mandarine tangerine
Mandeln almonds
Marillenknödel apricot dumplings (Austria)
Marmelade jam
Maronitorte chestnut tart
Märzenbier stronger beer brewed for special occasions
Mastochsenhaxe knuckle of beef (with sauce) from Sachsen-Anhalt (East German)
Maß a litre of beer
Matjes herring
Maultaschen ravioli-like pasta filled with pork, veal and spinach mixture
Meeresfrüchte seafood
Meerrettich horseradish
Mehrkornbrötchen rolls made with several kinds of wholemeal flour
Melange milky coffee
Melone melon

Menü combination of items from the menu at a special price, usually consisting of three courses

Mettenden sausage with a filling similar to mince

Milch milk

  Milchrahmstrudel strudel filled with egg custard and soft cheese

  Milchreis rice pudding

  Milchshake milk shake

Mineralwasser mineral water

  mit/ohne Kohlensäure carbonated/non-carbonated

Mirabellen small yellow plums

Mischbrot grey bread made with rye and wheat flour

Mittagstisch lunch menu

Mohn poppy seed

  Mohnnudeln noodles with poppy seeds, cinnamon, sugar and butter

  Mohntorte gâteau with poppy seeds

Möhren carrots

  Möhrensalat carrot salad

Mohr im Hemd chocolate pudding

Most fruit juice; (in the South) fruit wine

Münchener a kind of dark lager from Munich

Muscheln mussels

Nachspeisen desserts

Nachtisch dessert

Nieren kidneys

Nierstein village on the Rhine producing medium to sweet white Rheinwein

Nockerln small dumplings

Nudeln noodles

Nudelsuppe noodle soup

Nüsse nuts

Nusskuchen nut cake

Nusstorte nut gâteau

Obst fruit

Obstkuchen fruit cake

Obstsalat fruit salad

Ochsenschwanz oxtail

Ochsenschwanzsuppe oxtail soup

Öl oil

Oppenheim village on the Rhine producing fine white wines

Orange orange

Orangensaft orange juce

Palatschinken pancakes filled with curd mixture or jam or ice cream

Pampelmuse grapefruit

paniert coated with breadcrumbs

Paprika bell pepper; paprika

Pellkartoffeln small boiled potatoes served in their skins, often with Quark

Peperoni hot chilli pepper

Petersilie parsley

Pfannkuchen pancake
Pfeffer pepper
  Pfefferkäse mit Schinken ham and pepper cheese log
Pfifferlinge chanterelles
Pfirsich peach
Pflaumen plums
  Pflaumenkuchen plum tart
Pils, Pilsner a strong, slightly bitter lager
Pilze mushrooms
Pilzsuppe mushroom soup
Pommes frites chips
Portion portion, serving
Powidltascherl ravioli-like pasta filled with plum jam (Austria)
Preiselbeeren cranberries
Pumpernickel very dark bread made with coarse wholemeal rye flour
Punschpudding pudding containing alcohol
Pute turkey
  Puten-schnitzel turkey breast in breadcrumbs

Quark curd cheese

Raclette melted cheese and potatoes
Radieschen radish(es)
Radler beer with lemonade, shandy
Ragout stew
Rahm cream

Rahmschnitzel escalope with a creamy sauce
Rahmsuppe creamy soup
Räucherkäse mit Schinken smoked cheese with bacon pieces in it
Räucherkäse mit Walnüssen smoked cheese with pieces of walnut in it
Räucherlachs smoked salmon
Räucherspeck smoked bacon
Reh venison
  Rehrücken roast saddle of venison
Reibekuchen potato cakes
Reis rice
Remoulade, Remouladensauce tartar sauce
Rhabarber rhubarb
Riesling Riesling wine
  Rieslingsuppe wine soup made with Riesling
Rind(fleisch) beef
  Rinderbraten roast beef
  Rinderrouladen rolled beef (beef olives)
Rippenbraten roast spare ribs
Risi lisi, Risibisi rice with peas
roh raw
Rollmops marinated herring fillets rolled up with onion, gherkins and white peppercorns
Rosenkohl Brussels sprouts
Roséwein rosé wine
Rosinen raisins
Rösti fried diced potatoes, onions and bacon
Rotbarsch rosefish

rote Bete beetroot
rote Grütze raspberry, redcurrant and wine jelly
rote Rübe beetroot
Rotkohl red cabbage
Rotwein red wine
Roulade beef olive
Rübe turnip
Rührei scrambled eggs

Sachertorte rich chocolate gâteau
Saft juice
Sahne cream
Saison season, e.g. **je nach Saison** = depending
  on the season
Salat salad
  gemischter Salat mixed salad
  Salatbeilage side salad
Salz salt
Salzkartoffeln boiled potatoes
Sardellen anchovies
Sardinen sardines
Sauerbraten braised pickled beef served with
  dumplings and vegetables
Sauerkraut shredded pickled white cabbage
Scampi scampi
Schafskäse ewe's milk cheese
scharf spicy
Schaschlik shish kebab
Schellfisch haddock

Schnaps strong spirit
Schinken ham
  Schinkenkipferl ham-filled croissant
  Schinkenwurst ham sausage
Schlachtplatte platter of cold meat and sausage
Schlagsahne whipped cream
Schmelzkäse cheese spread
Schmorgurken hotpot with cucumber and meat
Schnecke snail
Schnittlauch chives
  Schnittlauchbrot chives on bread
Schnitzel escalope
Schokolade chocolate
Schokoladentorte chocolate gâteau
Scholle plaice
Schorle wine and sparkling water
Schwäbischer Apfelkuchen apple cake from Swabia
Schwammerlgulasch mushroom stew
Schwarzbrot rye bread
schwarze Johannisbeeren blackcurrants
schwarzer Tee black tea
Schwarzwälder Kirschtorte Black Forest cherry gâteau
Schwarzwälder Schinken Black Forest ham
Schwarzwälder Torte fruit compote flan with cream
Schwein pork
  Schweinebraten roast pork

Schweinefleisch pork
Schweinekotelett pork chop
Schweinshaxe knuckle of pork
Schweinsrostbraten roast pork
Schwertfisch swordfish
Seezunge sole
Sekt sparkling wine
Selters(wasser) sparkling mineral water
Semmeln bread rolls
Semmelknödel bread dumpling
Senf mustard
Seniorenteller small portion for senior citizens
Sesam sesame
Scampi scampi
Sliwowitz plum brandy
Sonnenblumenbrot wholemeal bread with
 sunflower seeds
Soße sauce
Spanferkel suckling pig
Spargel asparagus
 Spargelcremesuppe cream of asparagus soup
 Spargelsalat asparagus salad
Spätzle home-made noodles
Speck bacon (fat)
Speisekarte (printed) menu
Spezialität des Hauses speciality of the
 house/chef's special
Spiegelei fried egg, sunny side up
Spieß kebab style

Spinat spinach
Sprudel sparkling mineral water
Stachelbeeren gooseberries
Stachelbeertorte gooseberry tart
Stangl croissant covered with cheese
Starkbier strong beer
Steinbutt turbot
Steinpilze porcini
Steirischer Selchkäse ewe's milk cheese (Austria)
Steirisches Lammkarree mit Basilikum lamb
  baked with basil (Austria)
Sterz Austrian polenta
Stollen spiced loaf with candied peel traditionally
  eaten at Christmas
Strudel strudel
Sulz/Sülze aspic
Suppen soups
süß sweet
süßsauer sweet-and-sour

Tafelspitz boiled beef of various cuts
Tafelspitzsulz beef in aspic
Tagesgericht dish of the day
Tagessuppe soup of the day
Tee tea
  Tee mit Milch tea with milk
  Tee mit Zitrone tea with lemon
  eine Tasse Tee a cup of tea
  ein Kännchen Tee a (small) pot of tea

Thunfisch tuna fish
Thüringer Rostbratwurst sausages from
  Thuringia, grilled or fried
Tilsiter savoury cheese with sharpish taste
Tintenfisch squid
Tomaten tomatoes
  Tomatensaft tomato juice
  Tomatensoße tomato sauce
Topf stew
Topfen curd cheese (Austria)
  Topfenstrudel flaky pastry strudel with curd-
  cheese filling
Torte gâteau
Trauben grapes
  Traubensaft grape juice
trocken dry (wine)
Truthahn turkey
Türkischer Kaffee Turkish coffee

überbacken au gratin
vegetarische Gerichte vegetarian dishes

Vollkorn wholemeal
Vollkornbrot wholemeal bread
Vorspeisen starters

Wacholder juniper
Waldpilze wild mushrooms
Walnüsse walnuts

warm warm

warmer Krautsalat salad with warm cabbage and crunchy bacon

Wasser water

Weichkäse cream cheese

Wein wine

Weinbrand brandy

Weinkarte wine list

Weißbrot wheat bread

Weiße golden wheat beer

Weißkohl white cabbage

Weißwein white wine

Weißwurst white sausage (veal and pork with herbs)

Weizenbier wheat beer

Wels catfish

Westfälischer Schinken Westphalian ham

Wiener frankfurters

Wiener Backhendl roast chicken covered in breadcrumbs

Wiener Fischfilets fish fillets baked in a sour cream sauce

Wiener Hofburgtorte chocolate gâteau

Wiener Kartoffelsuppe potato soup with mushrooms

Wiener Schnitzel veal escalope fried in breadcrumbs

Wiener Würstchen frankfurter

Wild game

Wildbraten roast venison

Wildgulasch game stew with paprika
Wildschwein wild boar
Wirsingkohl Savoy cabbage
Wurst sausage
Würstchen frankfurter
Würzfleisch strips of meat roasted in a spicy sauce

Zander pike-perch
Ziegenkäse goat's cheese
Ziegett mixed milk cheese
Zigeunerschnitzel escalope in paprika sauce
Zillertaler cow's cheese from the Zillertal
Zimt cinnamon
Zitrone lemon
  Zitronentee lemon tea
Zopf braided bread loaf
Zucchini courgette
Zucker sugar
Zuger Köteli baked dace with herbs and wine
Zunge tongue
Zürcher Geschnetzeltes thinly sliced meat
  (veal or turkey), served with a wine sauce and
  mushrooms
Zwetschgen plums
  Zwetschgendatschi damson tart
Zwiebeln onions
  Zwiebelkuchen onion flan
  Zwiebelrostbraten large steak with onions

Grammar

Nouns

••

In German all nouns begin with a capital letter. The plural form varies from noun to noun: there is no universal plural as in English (cat – cats, dog – dogs):

singular	plural
Mann	**Männer**
Frau	**Frauen**
Tisch	**Tische**

In the Dictionary, plural forms appear where they may be useful.

German nouns are masculine *(m)*, feminine *(f)* or neuter *(nt)*, and this is shown by the words for *the* and *a(n)* used before them:

	masculine	feminine	neuter
the	**der Mann**	**die Frau**	**das Licht**
a, an	**ein Mann**	**eine Frau**	**ein Licht**

The plural of *the* for all nouns is **die**:
    die Männer   die Frauen   die Lichter

There is no plural of **ein**: the plural noun is used on its own.

From the phrases in this book you will see that the endings of the words for *the* and *a(n)* vary according to the part the noun plays in a sentence.

Several other words used before nouns have similar endings to **der** and **ein**.

Those like **der** are:
    dieser this; **jener** that; **jeder** each;
    welcher which

Those like **ein** are:
    mein my; **dein** your (informal sing.);
    Ihr your (formal sing. and plural); **sein** his;
    ihr her; **unser** our; **euer** your (informal plural);
    ihr their

The word **kein** (no, not any) also has the same endings as **ein**, except that it can be used in the plural:
    keine Männer

Adjectives

When adjectives are used before a noun, their endings vary like the words for **der** and **ein**, depending on the gender (masculine, feminine or neuter), whether the noun is plural, and how the noun is used in the sentence (whether it is the subject, object, etc.). Here are examples using the adjective **klug** – clever:

	with der	with ein
Masculine	**der kluge Mann**	**ein kluger Mann**
Feminine	**die kluge Frau**	**eine kluge Frau**
Neuter	**das kluge Kind**	**ein kluges Kind**
Plural	**die klugen Kinder**	**klugen Kinder**

When the adjective follows the verb, there is no agreement:

der Mann ist klug; die Frau ist klug;
das Kind ist klug

My, your, his, her...

•••

These words all take the same endings as **ein**, and they agree with the noun they accompany, i.e. whether masculine, feminine, neuter or plural, and according to the function of the noun in the sentence:

mein Mann kommt my husband is coming (subject)

ich liebe meinen Mann I love my husband (object)

meine Frau kommt my wife is coming

meine Kinder kommen my children are coming (nom. pl.)

Other words which take these endings are:

dein	your (informal sing.)
sein	his
ihr	her
unser	our
euer	your (informal plural)
Ihr	your (formal singular and plural)
ihr	their

subject		direct object	
I	ich	**me**	mich
you (informal sing.)	du	**you** (informal sing.)	dich
he/it	er	**him/it**	ihn
she/it	sie	**her/it**	sie
it (neuter)	es	**it** (neuter)	es
we	wir	**us**	uns
you (informal pl.)	ihr	**you** (informal pl.)	euch
you (form. sing. & pl.)	Sie	**you** (form. sing. & pl.)	Sie
they (all genders)	sie	**them** (all genders)	sie

Pronouns

Indirect object pronouns are:
   to me **mir**; to you (informal sing.) **dir**;
   to him/it **ihm**; to her/it **ihr**; to it (neuter) **ihm**;
   to us **uns**; to you (informal plural) **euch**; to you
   (formal sing. and plural) **Ihnen**; to them **ihnen**

There are two ways of addressing people in German: informal and formal. The informal forms are **du** (used when talking to just one person you know well) and **ihr** (used when talking to more than one person you know well). The formal form is **Sie** (always written with a capital letter), which can be used to address one or more people.

Verbs

There are two main types of verb in German: weak verbs (which are regular) and strong verbs (which are irregular).

	weak		**strong**	
	spielen	**helfen**	**sein**	**haben**
	to play	to help	to be	to have
ich	spiele	helfe	bin	habe
du	spielst	hilfst	bist	hast
er/sie/es	spielt	hilft	ist	hat
wir	spielen	helfen	sind	haben
ihr	spielt	helft	seid	habt
Sie	spielen	helfen	sind	haben
sie	spielen	helfen	sind	haben

To make a verb negative, add **nicht**:

ich verstehe nicht I don't understand
das funktioniert nicht it doesn't work

Past tense

Here are a number of useful past tenses:

ich war	I was
wir waren	we were
Sie waren	you were (formal)
ich hatte	I had
wir hatten	we had
Sie hatten	you had (formal)
ich/er/sie/es spielte	I/he/she/it played
Sie/wir/sie spielten	you/we/they played
ich/er/sie/es half	I/he/she/it helped
Sie/wir/sie halfen	you/we/they helped

Another past form corresponds to the English or
'*have ...ed*' and uses the verb **haben** 'to have':

ich habe gespielt	I have played
wir haben geholfen	we have helped

Future

In German the present tense is very often used where we would use the future tense in English:

ich schicke ein Fax   I will send a fax
ich schreibe einen Brief   I will write a letter

Public holidays

••••••••••••••••••••••••••••••••••••

Only German public holidays are listed here: those in
Austria and Switzerland differ. The holidays marked *
are not observed in all regions of Germany.

January 1	**Neujahr**	New Year's Day
January 6*	**Heilige Drei Könige**	Epiphany
March/April	**Karfreitag**	Good Friday
	Ostersonntag	Easter Day
	Ostermontag	Easter Monday
May	**Erster Mai/Maifeiertag**	
	May Day/Labour Day	
May/June	**Christi Himmelfahrt**	Ascension
May/June	**Pfingstsonntag**	Whit Sunday
	Pfingstmontag	Whit Monday
May/June*	**Fronleichnam**	Corpus Christi
August 15*	**Mariä Himmelfahrt**	Assumption
October 3	**Tag der deutschen Einheit**	
	Day of German Unity	
October 31*	**Reformationstag**	Day of Reformation
November 1*	**Allerheiligen**	All Saints' Day
November*	**Buß- u. Bettag**	Day of Repentance
December 25	**Erster Weihnachtstag**	
	Christmas Day	
December 26	**Zweiter Weihnachtstag/**	
	Stephanstag	Boxing Day/
	St Stephen's Day	

English - German

A

a	ein, eine	yn, **yn**-e
able: *to be able*	können	**kur**'nen
about (concerning)	über	**ue**ber
above (overhead)	oben	**oh**ben
(higher than)	über	**ue**ber
abroad	im Ausland	im **ows**lant
to accept	akzeptieren	ak-tsep**teer**-ren
accident	der Unfall	**oon**fal
accommodation	die Unterkunft	**oon**terkoonft
to accompany	begleiten	be**gly**ten
account (bill)	die Rechnung	**rekh**'noong
to ache: *it aches*	es tut weh	es toot **veh**
address	die Adresse	a-**dres**-e
admission fee	der Eintrittspreis	**ynt**rits-prys
adult	der/die Erwachsene	er**vak**-se-ne
advance: *in advance*	im Voraus	im **fohr**ows
to advise	raten	**rah**ten

afraid: *to be afraid of*	Angst haben vor	angst **hah**ben fohr
after (afterwards)	danach	da**nahkh**
after lunch	nach dem Mittagessen	nahkh dem **mittahk**-essen
afternoon	der Nachmittag	**nahkh**-mittahk
again	wieder	**vee**der
against	gegen	**geh**gen
age	das Alter	**al**ter
ago: *a week ago*	vor einer Woche	fohr **yn**-er **vokh**-e
to agree	vereinbaren	fer-**yn**bahren
air	die Luft	looft
air conditioning	die Klimaanlage	**kleema**-anlähge
air mail: *by air mail*	per Luftpost	per **looft**post
airplane	das Flugzeug	**flook**-tsoyk
airport	der Flughafen	**flook**-hahfen
airport bus	der Flughafenbus	**flook**-hahfen-boos

English	German	Pronunciation
air ticket	das Flugticket	flook-tikket
alarm call	der Weckruf	vekroof
alarm clock	der Wecker	vekker
alcohol	der Alkohol	alko-**hohl**
alcohol-free	alkoholfrei	alko-**hohl**fry
alcoholic	alkoholisch	alko-**hohl**ish
all	alle	**al**-e
allergic: to be allergic to	allergisch sein gegen	a-**ler**-gish zyn **geh**gen
allergy	die Allergie	a-ler-**gee**
to allow	erlauben	er**low**ben
to be allowed	dürfen	**duer**fen
all right (agreed)	in Ordnung	in **ort**-noong
almost	fast	fast
alone	allein	a-**lyn**
Alps	die Alpen	**alp**en
already	schon	shohn
also	auch	owkh
always	immer	**imm**er
a.m. (small hours)	nachts	nakhts
(morning)	vormittags	**fohr**-mittahks

English	German	Pronunciation
America	Amerika	a**mehr**ika
American adj	amerikanisch	amehri**kah**nish
amount: total amount	die Gesamtsumme	ge**zamt zoom**-e
and	und	oont
angry	zornig	**tsorn**ikh
animal	das Tier	teer
annual	jährlich	**yehr**likh
answer	die Antwort	**ant**vort
to answer	antworten	**ant**vorten
any	jeglicher(r/s)	**yehk**-likh-e
anybody	jeder	**yehd**er
anything	irgendetwas	**irg**ent-**et**vas
anywhere	irgendwo	**irg**ent-voh
apartment	das Appartement	a-**par**-te-ment
appointment	der Termin	ter**meen**
approximately	ungefähr	**oon**-ge-fehr
arm	der Arm	arm
to arrest	verhaften	fer**haf**ten
arrival	die Ankunft	**an**koonft
to arrive	ankommen	**an**kommen

English - German

English	German	Pronunciation
art gallery	die Kunsthalle	koonsthalle
artist	der/die Künstler(in)	kuenstler(in)
to ask (question)	fragen	frahgen
(for something)	bitten um	bitten oom
asleep:		
to be asleep	schlafen	shlahfen
to fall asleep	einschlafen	yn-shlahfen
atm	der Geldautomat	gelt-owtoh-maht
audience	das Publikum	pooblikoom
aunt	die Tante	tan-te
Australia	Australien	owstrah-li-en
Australian adj	australisch	owstrahlish
Austria	Österreich	ur'ster-rykh
Austrian adj	österreichisch	ur'ster-rýkhish
automatic	automatisch	owtoh-mahtish
available	erhältlich	erheltlikh
awake	wach	vakh
away	weg	vek
awful	schrecklich	shrekklikh

B

English	German	Pronunciation
baby	das Baby	bee
back (of body, hand)	der Rücken	ruekken
backpack	der Rucksack	rooksak
bacon	der Speck	shpek
bad (weather, etc.)	schlecht	shlekht
(fruit, vegetables)	verdorben	ferdorben
bag	die Tasche	tash-e
baggage allowance	das Freigepäck	fry-gepek
baked	gebacken	gebakken
baker's	die Bäckerei	bek-e-ry
Baltic Sea	die Ostsee	ostzeh
bank	die Bank	bank
bank account	das Bankkonto	bankkontoh
banknote	der Geldschein	geltshyn
barbecue	der Grill	gril
Basle	Basel	bahzel
bath	das Bad	baht

English	German	Pronunciation
tub	die Badewanne	**bah**-de-van-ne
to have a bath	ein Bad nehmen	yn baht **nehm**en
bathroom	das Badezimmer	**bah**-de-**tsimmer**
battery	die Batterie	ba-te-**ree**
to be	sein	zyn
beach	der Strand	shtrant
beautiful	schön	shur'n
because	weil	vyl
to become	werden	vehrden
bed	das Bett	bet
bed and breakfast	Übernachtung mit Frühstück	**ueber**nakht-oong mit **frue**shtuek
bedroom	das Schlafzimmer	**shlahf**-tsimmer
beef	das Rindfleisch	rintflysh
beer	das Bier	beer
before	vor	fohr
to begin	beginnen	be**ginn**en
behind	hinter	**hint**er
to belong to	gehören zu	gehur'-en tsoo
below	unterhalb	**oont**erhalb
beside (next to)	neben	**neh**ben
better than	besser als	**bess**er als
between	zwischen	**tsvi**shen
bicycle: by bicycle	mit dem Fahrrad	mit dehm **fahr**raht
big	groß	grohs
bigger than	größer als	**grur'**ser als
bill (account)	die Rechnung	**rekh**noong
bin (dustbin)	der Mülleimer	**muel**-ymer
bird	der Vogel	**foh**gel
birthday	der Geburtstag	ge**boorts**tahk
biscuits	die Kekse	**kehk**-se
bit (piece)	das Stück	shtuek
a bit (a little)	ein bisschen	yn **bis**khen
bite (by insect)	der Biss	bis
bitten (by insect)	gestochen	ge-**shtokh**-en
black	schwarz	shvarts
to bleed	bluten	**bloo**ten

English	German	Pronunciation
blind (person)	blind	blint
blister	die Blase	**blah**-ze
blond (person)	blond	blont
blood pressure	der Blutdruck	**bloot**-drook
blouse	die Bluse	**bloo**-ze
to blow-dry	föhnen	**fur**'nen
blue	blau	blow
blunt (blade)	stumpf	shtoompf
to board (plane, train, etc)	einsteigen	**yn**-stygen
boarding card/pass	die Bordkarte	**bort**kar-te
boat (large)	das Schiff	shif
boat (small)	das Boot	boht
boat trip	die Bootsfahrt	**bohts**fahrt
boiled	gekocht	ge**kokht**
book	das Buch	bookh
to book	buchen	**boo**-khen
booking (in hotel, train, etc)	die Reservierung	re-zer-**veer**-roong

bookshop	die Buchhandlung	**bookh**-hantloong
boots	die Stiefel	**shtee**fel
boring	langweilig	**lang**vilikh
born	geboren	ge**boh**ren
to borrow	borgen	**bor**gen
boss	der/die Chef(in)	shef(in)
both	beide	**by**-de
bottle	die Flasche	**flash**-e
box office	die Kasse	**kas**-e
boy	der Junge	**yoong**-e
boyfriend	der Freund	froynt
bread	das Brot	broht
brown bread	Schwarzbrot	**shvarts**broht
sliced bread	geschnittenes Brot	ge**shnitt**-e-nes broht
white bread	Weißbrot	**vys**broht
bread roll	das Brötchen	**brur't**-khen
to break (object)	zerbrechen	tser**brekh**en
breakdown (car)	die Panne	**pan**-e
breakfast	das Frühstück	**frue**shtuek

bridge	die Brücke	**brue**-ke
briefcase	die Aktentasche	**akten**-tash-e
to bring	bringen	**bring**-en
Britain	Großbritannien	grohs**brita**-ni-en
British	britisch	**british**
broadband	das Breitband	**brytbant**
brochure	die Broschüre	bro**shue**-re
broken	gebrochen	ge**brokhen**
broken down (car, etc)	kaputt	ka**poot**
brother	der Bruder	**broo**der
brown	braun	brown
buffet car	der Speisewagen	**shpy**-ze-**vah**gen
to build	bauen	**bow**en
building	das Gebäude	ge**boy**-de
burger	der Hamburger	**ham**boorger
bus	der Bus	boos
bus station	der Busbahnhof	**boos**-bahn-hohf
bus stop	die Bushaltestelle	**boos**-hal-te-shtel-e

bus ticket	der Busfahrschein	**boos**-fahr-shyn
bus tour	die Busfahrt	**boos**fahrt
business	das Geschäft	ge**sheft**
on business	geschäftlich	ge**sheft**likh
business card	die Visitenkarte	vi**zeeten**-kar-te
business trip	die Geschäftsreise	ge**shefts**-ry-ze
busy	beschäftigt	be**shef**ikht
but	aber	**aber**
butcher's	die Fleischerei	fly-she-**ry**
to buy	kaufen	**kow**fen
by (beside)	bei	by
(via)	über	**ueber**
by bus	mit dem Bus	mit dehm boos

C

cake	der Kuchen	**kook**hen
cake shop	die Konditorei	kon-di-to-**ry**
call (on phone)	der Anruf	**anroof**
to call (on phone)	anrufen	**anroof**en

English – German

English	German	Pronunciation
calm (person) (weather)	ruhig	**roo**ikh
(weather)	windstill	**vint**shtill
to camp	campen	**kem**pen
campsite	der Campingplatz	**kem**pingplats
can (to be able)	können	**kur'**nen
Canada	Kanada	**ka**nada
Canadian adj	kanadisch	ka**nah**dish
to cancel	stornieren	shtor**neer**-ren
cancellation	die Stornierung	shtor**neer**-roong
car	das Auto	**ow**toh
car ferry	die Autofähre	**ow**toh-feh-re
car park	der Parkplatz	**park**plats
careful	vorsichtig	**fohr**zikh-tikh
be careful!	passen Sie auf!	**pass**en zee owf!
to carry	tragen	**trah**gen
case (suitcase)	der Koffer	**koff**er
cash	das Bargeld	**bahr**gelt
cash desk	die Kasse	**kas**-e
cash machine	der Geldautomat	**gelt**-owtoh-**maht**
castle	das Schloss	shlos
cat	die Katze	**kat**-se
to catch (bus, etc.)	nehmen	**neh**men
cathedral	der Dom	dohm
cent (euro)	der Cent	sent
centre	das Zentrum	**tsent**room
cereal (breakfast)	die Cornflakes	**korn**flehks
certain (sure)	sicher	**zikh**er
chair	der Stuhl	shtool
change (money)	das Wechselgeld	**veks**elgelt
to change	ändern	**en**dern
(bus, train, etc)	umsteigen	**oom**-stygen
to change money	Geld wechseln	gelt **veks**eln
to change clothes	sich umziehen	zikh **oom** -tsee-en
changing room	die Umkleidekabine	**oom**-kly-de-kabee-ne
charge (fee)	die Gebühr	ge**buer**
to charge (battery)	aufladen	**owf**laden
(money)	berechnen	be**rekh**nen

English	German	Pronunciation
charge card (for mobile phone)	die Guthabenkarte	goot-habben-kar-te
cheap	billig	billich
cheap rate	der Billigtarif	billikhta-reef
to check in (at hotel)	einchecken	yn-checken
	sich an der Rezeption anmelden	zikh an dehr re-tsep-tsiohn anmelden
cheers! (toast)	Prost!	prohst!
chef	der Koch/die Köchin	kokh/kur'khin
chemist's (for medicines)	die Drogerie die Apotheke	dro-ge-ree apo-teh-ke
cheque	der Scheck	shek
cheque card	die Scheckkarte	shek-kar-te
chicken	das Hühnchen	huenkhen
child	das Kind	kint
chips (French fries)	die Pommes frites	pomfrit
chocolate	die Schokolade	shokolah-de
chocolates	die Pralinen	praleenen
to choose	auswählen	owsvehlen
Christmas	Weihnachten	vynakhten
Christmas Eve	Heiligabend	hylikh-ahbent
church	die Kirche	kir-khe
cinema	das Kino	keenoh
city centre	das Stadtzentrum	shtat-tsentroom
clean	sauber	zowber
to clean	säubern	zoybern
clear	klar	klahr
client	der Kunde/die Kundin	koon-de/koondin
to climb (mountains)	klettern	klettern
to close	schließen	shlee-sen
closed	geschlossen	geshlossen
clothes	die Kleider	klyder
clothes shop	das Bekleidungsgeschäft	beklydoongs-gesheft
cloudy	bewölkt	bevur'lkt
coach (bus)	der Bus	boos

English - German

coach station	der Busbahnhof	**boos**-bahn-hohf	
coach trip	die Busreise	**boos**-ry-ze	
cocoa	der Kakao	kakow	
coffee	der Kaffee	kafeh	
cold	kalt	kalt	
Cologne	Köln	kur'ln	
colour	die Farbe	**far**-be	
colour film	der Farbfilm	**farb**film	
to come	kommen	**kom**men	
to come back	zurückkommen	tsoo**ruek**-kommen	
comfortable	bequem	be**kvehm**	
company (firm)	die Firma	**fir**ma	
compartment (in train)	Abteil	ab**tyl**	
to complain	sich beschweren	zikh be**shvehr**en	
complaint	die Beschwerde	be**shvehr**-de	
complete	vollständig	fol-**shten**dikh	
concession	die Ermäßigung	er-**mehs**i-goong	
conference	die Konferenz	kon-fe-**rents**	
to confirm	bestätigen	be-**shteh**ti-gen	
confirmation (flight, etc)	die Bestätigung	be-**shteh**ti-goong	
connection (train, etc)	die Verbindung	fer**bind**oong	
convenient: is it convenient?	passt das so?	past das zoh?	
to cook	kochen	**koch**en	
cooked	gekocht	ge**kokht**	
cookies	die Kekse	**kehk**-se	
cool	kühl	kuel	
copy (duplicate)	die Kopie	ko**pee**	
to copy	kopieren	ko**peer**-ren	
corridor	der Flur	floo-er	
cost (price)	die Kosten	**kost**en	
cotton	die Baumwolle	**bowm**wolle	
country	das Land	lant	
couple	das Paar	pahr	
a couple of...	ein paar...	yn pahr...	
courier service	Kurierdienst	koo**reer**deenst	

English	German	
course (of study)	der Kurs	koors
(of meal)	der Gang	gang
cousin	der Cousin/ die Cousine	koozeng/ koozee-ne
cover charge (in restaurant)	der Gedeckpreis	gedekprys
cow	die Kuh	koo
crafts	das Kunsthandwerk	koonst-hantverk
to crash	einen Unfall haben	yn-en oonfal haben
cream (lotion)	die Creme	krehm
cream (on milk)	die Sahne	zah-ne
cream cheese	der Frischkäse	frishkeh-ze
credit (on mobile phone)	das Gesprächs-guthaben	geshprekhs-goot-haben
credit card	die Kreditkarte	kredit-kar-te
to cross (road)	überqueren	ueberqvehren
crowded	überfüllt	ueberfuelt
cruise	die Kreuzfahrt	kroytsfahrt
to cry (weep)	weinen	vynen
cucumber	die Gurke	goor-ke
cup	die Tasse	tas-e
currency	die Währung	vehroong
custom (tradition)	der Brauch	browkh
customer	der Kunde/ die Kundin	koon-de/ koondin
customs (duty)	der Zoll	tsol
to cut	schneiden	shnyden
cutlery	das Besteck	beshtek
to cycle	Rad fahren	raht fahren
cycle track	der Radweg	rahtvehg

D

English	German	
daily (each day)	täglich	tehklikh
dairy products	die Milchprodukte	milkhpro-dook-te
damage	der Schaden	shahden
damp	feucht	foykht
to dance	tanzen	tantsen
dangerous	gefährlich	gefehrlikh
dark	dunkel	doong-kel

date of birth	das Geburtsdatum	ge**boorts**-**daht**oom
daughter	die Tochter	**tokh**ter
day	der Tag	tahk
dead	tot	toht
debit card	die Debitkarte	de**bit**-kar-te
debts	die Schulden	**shool**den
decaffeinated	koffeinfrei	koffeh-**een**fry
to declare: nothing to declare	nichts zu verzollen	nikhts tsoo fer**tsol**len
deep	tief	teef
to defrost	entfrosten	ent**fros**ten
to de-ice	enteisen	ent**ys**-en
delay	die Verspätung	fer-**shpeh**toong
delicatessen	das Feinkostgeschäft	**fyn**-kost-ge**sheft**
delicious	köstlich	**kur**stikh
deodorant	das Deo	**deh**-oh
to depart	abfahren	**ap**fahren

department store	das Kaufhaus	**kowf**hows
departure (plane)	die Abfahrt / der Abflug	ap**fahrt** / ap**flook**
deposit	die Anzahlung	antsahloong
dessert	der Nachtisch	**nahkh**-tish
to develop (photos)	entwickeln	ent**vikk**eln
diabetic (person)	der Diabetiker / die Diabetikerin	dee-**abeht**iker / dee-**abeht**iker-rin
dialling code	die Vorwahl	**fohr**vahl
dialling tone	der Wählton	**vehl**lohn
diarrhoea	der Durchfall	**doorkh**fal
dictionary	das Wörterbuch	**vur**-ter-bookh
to die	sterben	**shter**ben
diet	die Diät	di-**eht**
different	verschieden	fer**shee**den
difficult	schwierig	**shveer**-nikh
dining room	das Esszimmer	**es**-tsimmer

English	German	Pronunciation
dinner (evening meal)	das Abendessen	**ah**bent-essen
direct (route) (train, etc)	direkt	di**rekt**
directory (phone)	das Telefonbuch	tele**fohn**-booh
directory enquiries	die Auskunft	**ows**koonft
dirty	schmutzig	**shmoots**ikh
to disappear	verschwinden	fersh**vin**den
discount	der Rabat	ra**bat**
dish (food)	das Gericht	ge-**rikht**
disk	die Diskette	dis**ket**-e
disposable	wegwerfbar	**vek**verfbahr
to disturb	stören	**shtur**'-ren
diversion	die Umleitung	**oom**lytoong
divorced	geschieden	ge**shee**den
dizzy	schwindlig	**shvint**likh
to do	machen	**makh**en
doctor	der Arzt/ die Ärztin	artst/ **ehrtst**in
documents	die Dokumente	dok**oo**men-te
dog	der Hund	hoont
domestic (flight)	Inlands	**in**lants
door	die Tür	tuer
double bed	das Doppelbett	**dopp**elbet
double room	das Doppel-zimmer	**dopp**el-**tsimm**er
doughnut	der Berliner	ber**lee**ner
draught lager	das Fassbier	**fas**beer
to dress (get dressed)	sich anziehen	zikh **ant**see-en
dressing (for food)	die Soße	**zoh**-se
drink	das Getränk	ge**trenk**
to drink	trinken	**tring**ken
drinking water	das Trinkwasser	**trink**vasser
to drive	fahren	**fahr**en
driver (of car)	der Fahrer/ die Fahrerin	**fahr**er/ **fahr**er-rin
driving licence	der Führerschein	**fuer**-rer-shyn
dry	trocken	**trokk**en
to dry	trocknen	**trokk**nen
dry cleaner's	die Reinigung	**ry**nigoong

English – German

English - German

English	German	
during	während	vehrent
duty-free	zollfrei	tsolfry
duvet	die Bettdecke	betdek-e

E

each	jede(r/s)	yeh-de(r/s)
ear	das Ohr	ohr
earlier	früher	frue-er
early	früh	frue
east	der Osten	osten
Easter	Ostern	ohstern
easy	leicht	lykht
to eat	essen	essen
economy class	die Touristenklasse	tooristen-klas-e
egg	das Ei	y
electric razor	der Elektrorasierer	elektro-razeer-rer
elevator	der Fahrstuhl	fahrshtool
embassy	die Botschaft	bohtshaft
emergency	der Notfall	nohtfal
empty	leer	lehr
end	das Ende	en-de
engaged (marry)	verlobt	ferlohpt
(toilet, telephone)	besetzt	bezetst
enough	genug	genook
that's enough	es reicht	es rykht
enquiry desk	die Auskunft	owskoonft
entrance	der Eingang	yn-gang
entrance fee	der Eintrittspreis	yn-trits-prys
equal	gleich	glykh
equipment	die Ausrüstung	owsruestoong
error	der Fehler	fehler
escalator	die Rolltreppe	roltrep-e
to escape	entkommen	entkommen
essential	wesentlich	vehzentlikh
euro	der Euro	oyroh
euro cent	der Eurocent	oyrohsent
Europe	Europa	oyrohpa
European	europäisch	oyropeh-ish
evening	der Abend	ahbent
every (each)	jede(r/s)	yeh-de(r/s)

everyone	jeder	yehder
everything	alles	al-es
everywhere	überall	ueber-al
example: *for example*	zum Beispiel	tsoom byshpeel
excellent	ausgezeichnet	owsge-tsykhnet
except	außer	owser
excess baggage	das Übergepäck	ueber-gepek
to exchange (money)	tauschen	towshen
exchange rate	der Wechselkurs	vekselkoors
exciting	aufregend	owfrehgent
excuse me! (sorry)	Entschuldigung!	entshooldigoong!
exit	der Ausgang	owsgang
expenses	die Spesen	die shpehzen
expensive	teuer	toyer
to expire (ticket, etc)	ungültig werden	oon-gueltikh vehrden
to explain	erklären	erklehren

explanation	die Erklärung	erklehroong
express (train)	der Schnellzug	shnel-tsook
extra (spare)	übrig	uebrikh
(more)	noch ein/eine	nokh yn/yn-e
eye	das Auge	ow-ge

F

face	das Gesicht	gezikht
facilities	die Einrichtungen	yn-rikhtoong-en
to faint	ohnmächtig werden	ohnmekh-tikh vehrden
fair (hair)	blond	blont
(just)	gerecht	gerekht
fake	unecht	oon-echt
to fall	fallen	fallen
family	die Familie	fameel-ye
famous	berühmt	beruemt
far	weit	vyt
how far is it?	wie weit ist es?	vee vyt ist es?
fare (train, bus, etc)	der Fahrpreis	fahrprys

English – German

English – German

English	German	Pronunciation
farm	der Bauernhof	**bower**nhohf
fast	schnell	shnel
too fast	zu schnell	tsoo shnel
fat (big)	dick	dik
father	der Vater	**fah**ter
father-in-law	der Schwiegervater	shvee**ger**-**fah**ter
fault (defect)	der Fehler	**feh**ler
it wasn't my fault	das war nicht meine Schuld	das vahr nikht **myn**-e **shoolt**
favour	der Gefallen	ge**fall**en
favourite	Lieblings	**leeb**lings
to fax	faxen	**fak**sen
to feel	fühlen	**fue**len
I feel sick	mir ist schlecht	meer ist **shlekht**
feet	die Füße	**fue**-se
ferry	die Fähre	**feh**-re
to fetch (bring)	holen	**hoh**len
fever	das Fieber	**feeb**er
few: a few	ein paar	yn pahr
fiancé(e)	der/die Verlobte	ferl**ohp**te

English	German	Pronunciation
to fight	kämpfen	**kemp**fen
to fill	füllen	**fue**llen
to fill in (form)	ausfüllen	**ows**fuellen
to fill up (tank)	voll tanken	fol **tang**ken
fillet	das Filet	fi-**leh**
film	der Film	film
to find	finden	finden
fine (to be paid)	die Geldstrafe	**gelt**-shtrah-fe
finger	der Finger	**fing**-er
to finish	beenden	be-**enden**
fire exit	der Notausgang	**noht**owsgang
firm (company)	die Firma	**firma**
first	erste(r/s)	**ehrs**-te(r/s)
first aid	die erste Hilfe	**ehrs**-te **hil**-fe
first class (travel)	die erste Klasse	**ehrs**-te **klas**-e
first name	der Vorname	**fornah**-me
fish	der Fisch	fish
to fix	passen	passen
to fix	reparieren	repa**reer**-ren
fizzy	sprudelnd	**shprood**elnd
flat (level)	flach	flakh

English	German	Pronunciation
flat	die Wohnung	**voh**noong
flavour	der Geschmack	geshmak
what flavour?	welchen Geschmack?	**vel**-khen ge-**shmak**?
flight	der Flug	flook
floor (of building)	die Etage	etah-zhe
	der Boden	**boh**den
flowers	die Blumen	**bloo**men
flu	die Grippe	**grip**-e
foggy	neblig	**neh**blikh
to fold	falten	**fal**ten
to follow	folgen	**fol**gen
food	das Essen	**es**sen
foot: on foot	zu Fuß	tsoo foos
football	der Fußball	**foos**bal
for	für	fuer
forbidden	verboten	fer**boh**ten
foreigner	ausländisch	**ows**lendish
	der Ausländer/	**ows**lender/
	die Ausländerin	**ows**lender-rin
forest	der Wald	valt

English	German	Pronunciation
forever	für immer	fuer **immer**
to forget	vergessen	fer**gess**en
fork (for eating)	die Gabel	**gah**bel
form (document)	das Formular	formoo**lahr**
fragile	zerbrechlich	tser**brekh**-likh
France	Frankreich	**frank**-rykh
free (vacant)	frei	fry
(costing nothing)	umsonst	oom**sonst**
French adj	französisch	fran-**tsur**-zish
French beans	die grünen Bohnen	**grue**nen **boh**nen
French fries	die Pommes frites	pom frit
frequent	häufig	**hoy**fikh
fresh	frisch	frish
Friday	Freitag	**fry**tahk
fried	gebraten	ge**brah**ten
friend	der Freund/	froynt/
	die Freundin	**froyn**din
friendly	freundlich	**froynt**likh

from	von	fon
from England	aus England	ows **eng**-lant
front	die Vorderseite	**for**der-zy-te
in front of	vor	fohr
frozen	gefroren	gefro**ren**
fruit juice	der Fruchtsaft	der **frookht**saft
fuel (petrol)	das Benzin	ben**zeen**
full	voll	fol
I'm full	ich bin satt!	ikh bin zat!
fun	der Spaß	shpahs
funny (amusing)	komisch	**koh**mish
future	die Zukunft	**tsook**oonft
G		
gallery	die Galerie	ga-le-**ree**
game	das Spiel	shpeel
garage (for repairs)	die Werkstatt	**verk**shtat
(petrol station)	die Tankstelle	tank-**shtel**-e
garden	der Garten	**gar**ten
garlic	der Knoblauch	**knohb**-lowkh
generous	großzügig	**grohs**-tsuegikh

genuine	echt	ekht
German adj	deutsch	doytsh
Germany	Deutschland	**doytsh**lant
to get (to obtain)	bekommen	bekommen
to get in(to)	einsteigen	**yn**-stygen
(bus, etc)		
to get off (bus, etc)	aussteigen	**ows**-shtygen
gift	das Geschenk	ge**shenk**
gift shop	der Geschenkeladen	ge**sheng**-ke-**lah**den
girl	das Mädchen	**meht**-khen
girlfriend	die Freundin	**froyn**din
to give	geben	**geh**ben
to give back	zurückgeben	tsoo**ruek**-gehben
glass of water	ein Glas Wasser	yn glahs **vass**er
glasses	die Brille	**bril**-e
(spectacles)		
gluten-free	glutenfrei	**gloo**tenfry

English	German	Pronunciation
to go (on foot)	gehen	geh-en
(in car)	fahren	fahren
to go back	zurückgehen	tsooruek-geh-en
to go in	hineingehen	hinyn-geh-en
to go out	ausgehen	ows-geh-en
good	gut	goot
(pleasant)	schön	shur'n
good morning	guten Morgen	gooten morgen
good night	gute Nacht	goo-te nakht
grandchild	das Enkelkind	engkelkint
grandparents	die Großeltern	grohseltern
great (big)	groß	grohs
(wonderful)	großartig	grohsahrtikh
Great Britain	Großbritannien	grohsbri-ta-ni-en
green	grün	gruen
grey	grau	grow
ground floor	das Erdgeschoss	ert-geshos
guarantee	die Garantie	ga-rantee
guest	der Gast	gast
guesthouse	die Pension	penziohn
guide (tour guide)	der Fremdenführer/die Fremdenführerin	fremdenfuer-rer/fremden-fuer-rer-rin
guidebook	der Reiseführer	ry-ze-fuer-rer
guided tour	die Führung	fuer-roong

H

English	German	Pronunciation
hair	die Haare	hah-re
hairdresser	der Friseur	frizur
hairdryer	der Föhn	fur'n
half	halb	halp
a half bottle	eine kleine Flasche	yn-e kly-ne flash-e
half an hour	eine halbe Stunde	yn-e hal-be shtoon-de
half board	die Halbpension	halp-penziohn
half price	zum halben Preis	tsoom halben prys

English – German

English – German

ham (cooked)	der Schinken	shing-ken	we have...	wir haben...	veer **hah**ben...
(cured)	geräucherter Schinken	geroy-kherter **shing**ken	do you have...?	haben Sie...?	**hah**ben zee...?
hand	die Hand	hant	to have to	müssen	**muess**en
handbag	die Handtasche	**hant**-tash-e	he	er	ehr
hand luggage	das Handgepäck	**hant**-gepek	head	der Kopf	kopf
hangover	der Kater	kahter	headache	die Kopfschmerzen	**kopf**shmertsen
to hang up	auflegen	**owf**-lehgen	healthy	gesund	ge**zoont**
to happen	passieren	paseer-ren	to hear	hören	**hur'**-ren
what happened?	was ist passiert?	vas ist pa**seert**?	heart	das Herz	herts
happy	glücklich	**gluek**likh	heart attack	der Herzanfall	**herts**anfal
happy birthday!	alles Gute zum Geburtstag!	al-es **goo**-te tsoom ge**boorts**-tahk!	to heat up (food, milk)	aufwärmen	**owf**-vermen
Happy New Year!	ein gutes neues Jahr!	yn **goo**tes **noy**es yahr!	heating	die Heizung	**hyt**soong
harbour	der Hafen	**hah**fen	heavy	schwer	shvehr
hard (difficult)	schwierig	**shveer**-rikh	height	die Höhe	**hur'**-e
(not soft)	hart	hart	help!	Hilfe!	**hil**-fe!
to have	haben	**hah**ben	to help	helfen	**helf**en
I have...	ich habe...	ikh **hah**-be...	her	ihr/ihre	eer/**eer**-re
			to her	zu ihr	tsoo eer
			herbal tea	der Kräutertee	**kroy**tert-eh

English	German	Pronunciation
here	hier	heer
to hide	verstecken	fershtekken
high (number, speed)	hoch	hohkh
high	groß	grohs
high blood pressure	hoher Blutdruck	hoh-er blootdrook
him	ihm	eem
hire	die Vermietung	fermeetoong
to hire	mieten	meeten
hire car	das Mietauto	meet-owtoh
his	sein/seine	zyn/zyn-e
to hit	schlagen	shlahgen
to hold	halten	halten
(to contain)	enthalten	enthalten
holiday	der Feiertag	fyer-tahk
holidays	der Urlaub	oorlowp
on holiday	in den Ferien	in den feh-ri-en
home	Zuhause	tsoo how-ze
honest	ehrlich	ehrlikh
to hope	hoffen	hoffen
I hope so	hoffentlich	hoffentlikh
I hope not	hoffentlich nicht	hoffentlikh nikht
hospital	das Krankenhaus	krangken-hows
hot	heiß	hys
I'm hot	mir ist heiß	meer ist hys
it's hot (weather)	es ist heiß	es ist hys
hotel	das Hotel	hotel
hour	die Stunde	shtoon-de
half an hour	eine halbe Stunde	yn-e hal-be shtoon-de
house	das Haus	hows
how	wie	vee
how are you	wie geht es Ihnen	vee geht es eenen
how many	wie viele	vee feel-e
how much	wie viel	vee feel
hungry	hungrig	hoong-grikh
hurry: I'm in a hurry	ich habe es eilig	ikh hah-be es ylikh
to hurt	weh tun	veh toon
that hurts	das tut weh	das toot veh

English – German

English	German	Pronunciation
husband	der Mann	man
I	ich	ikh
ice	das Eis	ys
with/without ice	mit/ohne Eis	mit/**oh**-ne ys
ice cream	das Eis	ys
ice cube	der Eiswürfel	**ys**würfel
iced: *iced coffee*	der Eiskaffee	**ys**kafeh
idea	die Idee	ee**deh**
if	wenn	ven
ill	krank	krank
illness	die Krankheit	**krank**-hyt
immediately	sofort	zoh**fort**
to import	importieren	importeer-ren
important	wichtig	**vikh**tikh
impossible	unmöglich	oon**mur'g**likh
to improve	verbessern	fer**bess**ern
in	in	in
included	inbegriffen	**in**begriffen
inconvenient	unpassend	oonp...
to increase	vergrößern	fer-**gru...**
indoors	drinnen	**drinnen**
infection	die Infektion	infekt**siohn**
infectious	ansteckend	an**stekk**ent
information	die Auskunft	ows**koonft**
information	der Informations-	informa-
desk	schalter	tsiohns-**shal**ter
in front of	vor	fohr
ingredients	die Zutaten	**tsoo**tahten
inhaler (for medication)	der Inhalations-apparat	inhalat**siohns**-apa-**raht**
insect bite	der Insektenstich	in**zekten**-shtikh
insect repellent	das Insekten-schutzmittel	in**zekten**-shoots-mittel
inside	in	in
instead of	anstelle von	**an**-shtel-e fon
insurance	die Versicherung	fer**zikher**-roong
interesting	interessant	interess**ant**
international	international	internation**ahl**
(arrivals, etc.)	Ausland	**ows**lant

into	in	in
invitation	die Einladung	**yn**lahdoong
invoice	die Rechnung	**rekh**noong
Ireland	Irland	**ir**iant
Irish adj	irisch	**eer**ish
is	ist	ist
island	die Insel	**in**zel
it	es	es
Italian adj	italienisch	ital**yeh**nish
Italy	Italien	i**tah**li-en
to itch	jucken	**yook**ken

J

jacket	die Jacke	**yak**-e
jam (food)	die Marmelade	mar-me-**lah**-de
jammed	blockiert	blok**eert**
jealous	eifersüchtig	**y**ferzuekh-tikh
jeweller's	der Juwelier	yoo-ve-**leer**
jewellery	der Schmuck	shm**oo**k
job (employment)	die Stelle	**shtel**-e
to join in	mitmachen	**mit**makh-en

to joke	scherzen	**sherts**en
joke	der Witz	vits
journey	die Reise	**ry**-ze
juice	der Saft	saft
jumper	der Pullover	**poo**lohver
just: just two	nur zwei	noor tsvy
I've just arrived	ich bin gerade angekommen	ikh bin ge**rah**-de **an**-gekommen

K

to keep (retain)	behalten	be**halt**en
key	der Schlüssel	**shluess**el
keycard	die Schlüsselkarte	**shluess**el-kar-te
to kill	töten	**tur**'ten
kilometre	der Kilometer	kilo**meh**ter
kind (person)	nett	net
kiss	der Kuss	koos
kitchen	die Küche	**kue**khe
knife	das Messer	**mess**er

English – German

to know (facts)	wissen	**viss**en
(be acquainted with)	kennen	**kenn**en
I don't know	ich weiß nicht	ikh vys nikht
to know how	to können	**kur**'nen

L

lager	helles Bier	**hel**-es beer
bottled lager	Flaschenbier	**flash**enbeer
draught lager	Fassbier	**fass**beer
lake	der See	zeh
language	die Sprache	**shprah**-khe
large	groß	grohs
last (final)	letzte(r/s)	**lets**-te(r/s)
the last bus	der letzte Bus	dehr **lets**-te boos
last night	gestern Abend	**gestern ah**bent
last time	letztes Mal	**lets**-tes mahl
late	spät	shpeht
the train is late	der Zug hat Verspätung	der tsook hat fer-**shpeh**toong

later	später	**shpeh**
to laugh	lachen	**lakh**en
lazy	faul	fowl
to lead	führen	**fuer**-ren
lead-free	bleifrei	**bly**fry
to learn	lernen	**lern**en
when does the train leave?	weggehen/ wegfahren	**vek**geh-en/ **vek**fahren
	wann fährt der Zug ab?	van fehrt der tsook ap?
left: *on the left*	links	links
to the left	nach links	nahkh links
left-luggage	das Schließfach	**shlees**fakh
left-luggage office	die Gepäckauf- bewahrung	ge**pek**-**owf**-be- vahroong
leg	das Bein	byn
lemon tea	der Zitronentee	tsi**trohn**en-teh
lemonade	die Limonade	limo**nah**-de
less	weniger	**veh**niger
less than	weniger als	**veh**niger als

English		German
lesson	oonter-rikhts-shtoon-de	die Unterrichtsstunde
letter (written)	breef	der Brief
letterbox	breefkasten	der Briefkasten
library	bibliotehk	die Bibliothek
lie (untruth)	lue-ge	die Lüge
lift (elevator)	owftsook	der Aufzug
can I have a lift?	kur'nen zee mikh mitnehmen?	können Sie mich mitnehmen?
light (not heavy)	lykht	leicht
light	likht	das Licht
like (preposition)	vee	wie
to like	mur'gen	mögen
I like coffee	ikh tring-ke gern kafeh	ich trinke gern Kaffee
I don't like...	ikh mahg nikht/ kyn(-e)...	ich mag nicht/ keine(e)...
we'd like...	veer mur'khten...	wir möchten...
liqueur	likur	der Likör
to listen	tsoohur'-ren	zuhören
little (small)	klyn	klein

English		German
a little...	yn biskhen...	ein bisschen...
to live (exist)	lehben	leben
(reside)	vohnen	wohnen
I live in London	ikh voh-ne in london	ich wohne in London
living room	vohntsimmer	das Wohnzimmer
local (wine, speciality)	heezikh	hiesig
to lock	tsoo-shlee-sen	zuschließen
locker (luggage)	shleesfakh	das Schließfach
long	lang	lang
for a long time	lang-e tsyt	lange Zeit
to look after	zikh kuemmern oom	sich kümmern um
to look at	anshow-en	anschauen
to look for	zookhen	suchen
to lose	ferleer-ren	verlieren
lost (object)	ferlohren	verloren

English - German

English	German	Pronunciation
I've lost my wallet	ich habe meine Brieftasche verloren	ikh **hah**-be **myn**-e **breef**-tash-e fer**lohr**en
I'm lost (on foot)	ich habe mich verlaufen	ikh **hah**-be mikh fer**lowf**en
I'm lost (in car)	ich habe mich verfahren	ikh **hah**-be mikh fer**fahr**en
lost property office	das Fundbüro	**foont**-bue-roh
lot:		
a lot	viel	feel
loud	laut	lowt
lounge (in house)	das Wohnzimmer	**vohnt**simmer
love	die Liebe	**lee**-be
to love	lieben	**lee**ben
I love you	ich liebe dich	ikh **lee**-be dikh
I love swimming	ich schwimme gern	ikh **shvim**-e gern
lovely	schön	shur'n
low	niedrig	**need**rikh
low-alcohol	alkoholarm	alko-**hohl**arm
low-fat	fettarm	**fet**arm
luck	das Glück	gluek
lucky	glücklich	**gluek**likh
luggage	das Gepäck	ge**pek**
luggage trolley	der Gepäckwagen	ge**pek**vahgen
lunch	das Mittagessen	**mittahk**-essen
lunch break	die Mittagspause	**mittahks**-pow-ze
M		
mad	verrückt	fer-**ruekt**
magazine	die Zeitschrift	**tsyt**-shrift
maid (in hotel)	das Zimmermädchen	**tsimmer**-meht-khen
maiden name	der Mädchenname	**meht**-khen-nah-me
mail	die Post	post
by mail	per Post	per post
main (principal)	Haupt-	howpt

English	German		English	German	
main course (of meal)	das Hauptgericht **howpt**-ge-rikht		*what's the matter?*	was ist los?	vas ist lohs?
to make	machen	**makh**en	me (direct object)	mich	mikh
male	männlich	**men**likh	(indirect object)	mir	meer
man	der Mann	man	meat	das Fleisch	flysh
manager	der Geschäfts- führer/ die Geschäfts- führerin	ge**shefts**-fuer- rer/-rin	*I don't eat meat*	ich esse kein Fleisch	ikh **es**-e kyn flysh
			medicine	die Medizin	medi-**tseen**
many	viele	**fee**-le	medium rare (meat)	halb durch	halp doorkh
map (of region)	die Karte	**kar**-te	to meet	treffen	**treff**en
(of town)	die Landkarte	**lant**-kar-te	men	die Männer	**menn**er
	der Stadtplan	**shtat**plahn	to mend	reparieren	reparee**r**-ren
market place	der Marktplatz	**markt**plats	set menu	die Speisekarte	**shpy**-ze-kar-te
marmalade	die Orangen- marmelade	oranzhen-mar- me-**lah**-de	menu	die Tageskarte	**tah**-ges-kar-te
			message	die Nachricht	**nahkh**-rikht
married	verheiratet	fer**hy**rahtet	middle	die Mitte	**mit**-e
to marry	heiraten	**hy**rahten	milk	die Milch	milkh
matter: *it doesn't matter*	macht nichts	makht nikhts	semi-skimmed milk	Halbfettmilch	**halp**fetmilkh

English – German

skimmed milk	Magermilch	**mah**germilkh
with/without milk	mit/ohne Milch	mit/**oh**-ne milkh
mind:		
I don't mind	es ist mir egal	es ist meer **egahl**
mineral water	das Mineralwasser	minerahlvasser
minute	die Minute	minoo-te
Miss	Fräulein; Frau	**froy**lyn; frow
to miss (train, etc)	verpassen	fer**passen**
missing (object)	verschwunden	
my son's missing	mein Sohn ist weg	myn zohn ist vek
mistake	der Fehler	**fehler**
mobile (phone)	das Handy	**hendee**
mobile number	die Handy-nummer	**hendee**-noommer
Monday	Montag	**mohn**tahk
money	das Geld	gelt
money order	die Postanweisung	**post**-anyzoong

month	der Monat	**moh**nat
more	mehr	mehr
more than	mehr als	mehr als
more wine	noch etwas Wein	nokh **et**vas vyn
morning	der Morgen	**morgen**
most: most of	meiste von	**my**-ste fon
mother	die Mutter	**moott**er
mother-in-law	die Schwiegermutter	**shvee**ger-mootter
motorbike	das Motorrad	mo**tohr**-raht
motorway	die Autobahn	**ow**tohbahn
mouth	der Mund	moont
to move	bewegen	be**veh**gen
Mr	Herr	her
Mrs	Ms Frau	frow
much	viel	feel
too much	zu viel	tsoo feel
Munich	München	**muen**khen
music	die Musik	moo**zeek**
must	müssen	**muess**en
I must	ich muss	ikh moos

we must	wir müssen	veer **muessen**
you mustn't	du darfst nicht	doo darfst nikht
my	mein/meine	myn/**myn**-e

N

name	der Name	**nah**-me
what is your name?	wie ist Ihr Name?	vee ist eer **nah**-me?
narrow	eng	eng
national	national	natsio**nahl**
nationality	die Nationalität	natsionali**teht**
natural	natürlich	na**tuer**liikh
nature	die Natur	na**toor**
near	nahe	**nah**-e
is it near?	ist es in der Nähe?	ist es in der **neh**-e?
necessary	notwendig	**noht**vendikh
to need	brauchen	**brow**-khen
I need...	ich brauche...	ikh **brow**-khe...
I need to go	ich muss gehen	ikh moos **geh**-en
never	nie	nee

new	neu	noy
news	die Nachrichten	**nahkh**riikhten
newsagent's	der Zeitungsladen	**tsy**toongs **lah**den
newspaper	die Zeitung	**tsy**toong
newsstand	der Zeitungskiosk	**tsy**toongs-kee-osk
New Year's Eve	Silvester	zil**vester**
New Zealand	Neuseeland	noy**zeh**lant
next	nächste(r/s)	**neh**-kste(r/s)
the next bus	der nächste Bus	dehr **neh**-kste boos
next week	nächste Woche	**neh**-kste **vokh**-e
next to	neben	**neh**ben
nice (person)	nett	net
nice (place, holiday)	schön	shur'n
night	die Nacht	nakht
at night	am Abend	am **ah**bent
last night	gestern Abend	**gestern ah**bent
tonight	heute Abend	**hoy**-te **ah**bent

no	nein	nyn
no thanks	nein danke	nyn **dang**-ke
no problem	kein Problem	kyn problehm
nobody	niemand	**nee**mant
noise	der Lärm	lerm
noisy	laut	lowt
it's very noisy	es ist sehr laut	es ist zehr lowt
non-alcoholic	alkoholfrei	alko-**hohl**fry
none	keine(r/s)	**kyn**-e(r/s)
non-smoking	Nichtraucher	**nikht**-row-kher
north	der Norden	**nor**den
Northern Ireland	Nordirland	nordirlant
North Sea	die Nordsee	**nort**zeh
nose	die Nase	**nah**-ze
not	nicht	nikht
nothing	nichts	nikhts
nothing else	nichts weiter	nikhts **vy**ter
novel	der Roman	ro**mahn**
now	jetzt	yetst
nowhere	nirgends	**nir**gends
nuclear	nookleh-**ahr**	

number	die Zahl	tsahl
nurse	die Krankenschwester/der Krankenpfleger	**krang**ken-**shves**ter/ **krang**ken-**pfleh**ger
nut (to eat)	die Nuss	noos

O

oats	der Hafer	**hah**fer
occupation (work)	der Beruf	be**roof**
ocean	der Ozean	**oh**-tseh-ahn
of	von	fon
a glass of water	ein Glas Wasser	yn glahs **vass**er
made of...	aus...	ows...
off (light, radio)	aus	ows
(rotten)	schlecht	shlekht
office	das Büro	bue-**roh**
off-season	die Nebensaison	**neh**ben-ze-zong
often	oft	oft
how often?	wie oft?	vee oft?
old	alt	alt

English	German	Pronunciation
how are you?	wie alt sind Sie?	vee alt zint zee?
I'm ... years old	ich bin ... Jahre	ikh bin ... **yah**-re
on (light, radio)	an	an
(on top of)	auf	owf
on time	pünktlich	**puenkt**likh
once	einmal	**yn**mahl
at once	sofort	zoh**fort**
only	nur	noor
open	geöffnet	ge-**ur'f**net
to open	öffnen	**ur'f**nen
opposite	gegenüber	gehgen-**ue**ber
opposite the bank	gegenüber der Bank	gehgen-**ue**ber der bank
quite the opposite	ganz im Gegenteil	gans im **geh**gen-tyl
optician's	der Optiker	**op**tiker
or	oder	**oh**der
orange (colour)	orange	**oran**-zhe
orange juice	der Orangensaft	**oran**zhen-zaft

English	German	Pronunciation
order (in restaurant)	die Bestellung	beshtel**loong**
to order (food)	bestellen	beshtellen
organic	organisch	or**gah**nish
other: the other one	der/die/das andere	der/dee/das **and**er-re
have you got any others?	haben Sie noch andere?	**hah**ben zee nokh **and**er-re?
our	unser/unsere	**oon**zer/ **oon**-zer-re
out (light, etc)	aus	ows
she's out	sie ist nicht da	zee ist nikht dah
out of order	kaputt	ka**poot**
outdoor	im Freien	im **fry**-en
outside	draußen	**drow**ssen
over (above)	über	**ue**ber
to overbook	überbuchen	ueber-**boo**-khen
to overcharge	zu viel berechnen	tsoo feel be**rekh**nen
overdone (food)	verkocht	fer**kokt**
to oversleep	verschlafen	fer**shlah**fen

English – German

English	German	Pronunciation
to owe	schulden	
I owe you...	ich schulde Ihnen...	ikh **shool**-de eenen...
you owe me...	Sie schulden mir...	zee **shoo**lden meer...
owner	der Besitzer/ die Besitzerin	be**zit**ser/ be**zit**ser-rin
P		
package	das Paket	pa**keht**
package tour	die Pauschalreise	pow**shahl**-ry-ze
page	die Seite	**zy**-te
paid	bezahlt	be**tsahlt**
I've paid	ich habe bezahlt	ikh **hah**-be be**tsahlt**
pain	der Schmerz	shmerts
painkiller	das Schmerzmittel	**shmerts**mittel
palace	der Palast	pa**last**
pale	blass	blas
pancake	der Pfannkuchen	**pfan**-kookhen
paper	das Papier	pa**peer**
paralysed	gelähmt	ge**lehmt**
parcel	das Paket	pa**keht**
pardon?	wie bitte?	vee **bit**-e?
I beg your pardon!	Entschuldigung!	entshooldi-**goong**!
parents	die Eltern	**el**tern
park	der Park	park
to park	parken	**park**en
parking ticket (fine)	der Strafzettel	**shtrahf**-tsettel
(to display)	der Parkschein	**park**shyn
partner (business)	der Geschäfts-partner/ die Geschäfts-partnerin	ge**shefts**-partner/ ge**shefts**-partner-rin
(boy/girlfriend)	der Partner/ die Partnerin	**part**ner/ **part**ner-rin
party (celebration)	die Party	par**tee**
passenger	der Passagier	passa-**zheer**
passport	der Reisepass	**ry**-ze-pas

English	German	Pronunciation
passport control	die Passkontrolle	**pas**kontroll-e
pasta	die Nudeln	**noo**deln
pastry (cake)	das Gebäck	ge**bek**
pavement	der Bürgersteig	**buer**-ger-styg
to pay	zahlen	**tsah**len
I'd like to pay	ich möchte zahlen	ikh **mur'kh**te **tsah**len
where do I pay?	wo kann ich bezahlen?	vo kan ikh be**tsah**len?
payment	die Bezahlung	be**tsah**loong
payphone	das Münztelefon	**muents**-telefohn
peace	der Frieden	**free**den
peak rate	der Höchsttarif	**hur'khst**-tareef
peanut allergy	die Erdnussallergie	**erd**-noos-al-er-gee
pen	der Füller	**fue**ller
pencil	der Bleistift	**bly**shtift
penfriend	der Brieffreund/die Brieffreundin	**breef**-froynt/**breef**-froyndin
pension	die Rente	**ren**-te
people	die Leute	**loy**-te
pepper (spice)	der Pfeffer	**pfe**ffer
per	pro	proh
per day	pro Tag	proh tahk
per hour	pro Stunde	proh **shtoon**-de
per person	pro Person	proh per**zohn**
perhaps	vielleicht	fee**lykht**
petrol	das Benzin	bent**seen**
unleaded petrol	bleifreies Benzin	**bly**fry-es bent**seen**
petrol station	die Tankstelle	**tank**shtel-e
pharmacy	die Apotheke	apo-**teh**-ke
to phone	telefonieren	telefo**neer**-ren
phone	das Telefon	tele**fohn**
by phone	per Telefon	per tele**fohn**
phonebox	die Telefonzelle	tele**fohn-tsel**-e
phonecard	die Telefonkarte	tele**fohn-kar**-te
phone directory	das Telefonbuch	tele**fohn**-bookh
photocopy	die Fotokopie	**foh**toh-ko**pee**
photograph	das Foto	**foh**toh

English – German

to take a photograph	fotografieren	**foh**toh-gra**feer**-ren
to pick (choose)	auswählen	**ows**vehlen
pickpocket	der Taschendieb	**tash**endeep
pie (sweet)	der Obstkuchen	**ohbst**koochen
(savoury)	die Pastete	pas**teh**te
piece	das Stück	shtuek
pig	das Schwein	shwyn
pillow	das Kopfkissen	**kopf**kissen
PIN number	die Geheimzahl; die PIN-Nummer	ge**hym**-tsahl; **pin**-noommer
pink	rosa	**roh**za
pity: *what a pity*	wie schade	vee **shah**-de
place	der Platz	plats
place of birth	der Geburtsort	ge**boorts**ort
plain (unflavoured)	einfach	**yn**fakh
plane (airplane)	das Flugzeug	**flook**-tsoyk
plastic (made of)	Plastik-	**plas**tik
platform (at station)	der Bahnsteig	**bahn**shtyg
which platform?	welcher Bahnsteig?	**vel**-kher **bahn**shtyg?
to play	spielen	**shpee**len
please	bitte	**bit**-e
pleased	erfreut	er**froyt**
pleased to meet you	sehr erfreut	zehr er**froyt**
p.m. (afternoon)	nachmittags	**nahkh**-mittahks
(evening)	abends	**ah**bents
poached (egg, fish)	pochiert	po**sheert**
poisonous	giftig	**gif**tikh
police (force)	die Polizei	poli**tsy**
polluted	verschmutzt	fer**shmootst**
pool	der Swimmingpool	**svimm**ingpool
poor	arm	arm
popular	beliebt	be**leept**
pork	das Schweinefleisch	**shvy**-ne-flysh
possible	möglich	**mur'g**likh

English	German	Pronunciation
post: *by post*	per Post	per post
postbox	der Briefkasten	**bref**kasten
postcard	die Ansichtskarte	an**zikhts**-kar-te
postcode	die Postleitzahl	**post**-lyt-tsahl
post office	das Postamt	**post**amt
to postpone	verschieben	fer**sheeb**en
potato	die Kartoffel	kartoffel
potato salad	der Kartoffelsalat	kartoffel-zalaht
to prefer	vorziehen	**fohr**-tsee-en
pregnant	schwanger	**shvang**-er
to prepare	vorbereiten	**fohr**be-ryten
prescription	das Rezept	re-**tsept**
present *(gift)*	das Geschenk	geshenk
pretty	hübsch	huebsh
price	der Preis	prys
price list	die Preisliste	**prys**liste
private	privat	pri**vaht**
prize	der Preis	prys
probably	wahrscheinlich	vahrsheynlikh
problem	das Problem	problehm
programme	das Programm	program

English	German	Pronunciation
prohibited	verboten	fer**bohten**
to promise	versprechen	fer-**sprekh**-en
to pronounce	aussprechen	**ows**-shprekh-en
how's it pronounced?	wie spricht man das aus?	vee shprikht man das ows?
to provide	zur Verfügung stellen	tsoor ferfue**goong shtellen**
public	öffentlich	**ur'f**-fent-likh
public holiday	der gesetzliche Feiertag	ge**zets**-likh-e **fy**ertahk
to pull	ziehen	**tsee**-en
to pull over *(car)*	anhalten	**an**halten
pullover	der Pullover	**pool**ohver
purple	violett	vee-oh-**let**
purse	der Geldbeutel	**gelt**boytel
to push	stoßen	**shtoh**-sen
to put *(place)*	stellen	**shtellen**
Q		
quality	die Qualität	kvali**teht**
quantity	die Quantität	kvanti**teht**

English – German

English – German

English	German	Pronunciation
to quarrel	streiten	**shtry**ten
quarter	das Viertel	**feer**tel
question	die Frage	**frah**-ge
queue	die Schlange	**an**-shteh-en
to queue	anstehen	shnel
quick(ly)	schnell	**rooikh**
quiet	ruhig	

R

railcard	die Bahncard	**bahn**-kaht
railway station	der Bahnhof	**bahn**-hohf
rain	der Regen	**rehg**en
to rain	regnen	**rehg**nen
it's raining	es regnet	es **rehg**net
raincoat	der Regenmantel	**rehg**en-**man**tel
raisins	die Rosinen	ro**zee**nen
rare (unique)	selten	**zel**ten
(steak)	blutig	**bloo**tikh
rash (skin)	der Ausschlag	**ows**-shlahk
rate (price)	der Preis	prys

English	German	Pronunciation
rate of exchange	der Wechselkurs	**vek**selkoors
raw	roh	roh
razor	der Rasierapparat	razeer-apa-**raht**
razor blades	die Rasierklingen	razeer-kling-en
to read	lesen	**leh**zen
ready	fertig	**fehr**rikh
real	echt	ekht
receipt	die Quittung	**kvitt**oong
reception (desk)	der Empfang; die Rezeption	empf**ang**; re-tsep-**tsiohn**
to recognize	erkennen	er**ken**nen
to recommend	empfehlen	emp**feh**len
to recycle	recyceln	ri-**sy**keln
red	rot	roht
refund	die Rückerstattung	**ruek**-er-shatt**oong**
to refund	rückerstatten	**ruek**-er-shatten
to refuse	ablehnen	a**pleh**nen

English	German	Pronunciation
to register (at hotel)	sich anmelden	zikh anmelden
to reimburse	entschädigen	ent-**shehdi**-gen
relation (family)	der/die Verwandte	fervant-te
to remember	sich erinnern	zikh er-**inern**
to remove	entfernen	ent-fernen
to rent	mieten	**meeten**
to repair	reparieren	repareer-ren
to repeat	wiederholen	veeder**hohlen**
to reply	antworten	antvorten
to report	berichten	berikhten
to require	benötigen	be-**nur**'ti-gen
reservation	die Reservierung;	re-zer-**veer**-roong;
	die Buchung	**boo**-khoong
to reserve	reservieren;	re-zer-**veer**-ren;
	buchen	**boo**-khen
to rest	ruhen	**roo**-en
restaurant car	der Speisewagen	shpy-ze-vahgen
retired	pensioniert	penzio-**neert**

English	German	Pronunciation
to return (in car)	zurückfahren	tsoo**ruek**-fahren
(on foot)	zurückgehen	tsoo**ruek**-geh-en
(goods)	zurückgeben	tsoo**ruek**-gehben
return ticket (train)	die Rückfahrkarte	**ruek**-fahr-**kar**-te
(plane)	das Rückflugticket	**ruek**flook-tikket
reverse charge call	das R-Gespräch	er-ge-**sh**prehkh
rich (person)	reich	rykh
(food)	reichhaltig	**rykh**-haltikh
right (correct)	richtig	**rikh**-tikh
right:		
on the right	rechts	rekhts
to the right	nach rechts	nahkh rekhts
ripe	reif	ryf
river	der Fluss	floos
road	die Straße	**shtrah**-se

English – German

English	German	Pronunciation
road map	die Straßenkarte	**shtrah**-sen-**kar**-te
roast	Rost-	rost
roll (bread)	das Brötchen	**brur't**-khen
romantic	romantisch	ro**man**tish
room (in house)	das Zimmer	**tsimmer**
(space)	der Platz	plats
room number	die Zimmernummer	**tsimmer**-noommer
room service	der Zimmerservice	**tsimmer**serservis
rose (flower)	die Rose	**roh**-ze
rotten (fruit, etc)	verfault	fer**fowlt**
round	rund	roont
rubbish	der Abfall	**ap**fal
rucksack	der Rucksack	**rook**zak
to run	rennen	**rennen**
rush hour	die Rushhour	**rash**-ower
rye bread	das Roggenbrot	**roggen**broht

S

English	German	Pronunciation
sad	traurig	**trow**rikh
safe (for valuables)	der Safe	seif
safe	ungefährlich	**oon**-ge-**fehrlikh**
to sail	segeln	**zeh**geln
salad	der Salat	za**laht**
green salad	grüner Salat	**gruener za**laht
mixed salad	gemischter Salat	ge**mishter** zalaht
salad dressing	die Salatsoße	za**laht**soh-se
salary	das Gehalt	ge**halt**
sale (in general)	der Verkauf	fer**kowf**
(seasonal)	Schlussverkauf	**shlooss**ferkowf
salesperson	der Verkäufer/die Verkäuferin	fer**koyfer/**ferkoyfer-rin
salt	das Salz	zalts
salty	salzig	**zalts**ikh
same	gleich	glykh
sandals	die Sandalen	zan**dahlen**
sandwich	das Sandwich	**sent**vitsh
Saturday	Samstag	**zams**-tahk

English	German	Pronunciation
sauce	die Soße	zoh-se
sausage	die Wurst	voorst
to save (money)	sparen	shpahren
savoury	pikant	pikant
scenery	die Landschaft	lantshaft
schedule	der Plan	plahn
school	die Schule	shoo-le
score	der Endstand	entshtant
Scotland	Schottland	shotlant
Scottish	schottisch	shottish
to see	sehen	zeh-en
selection	die Auswahl	owsvahl
	für	fuer
self-catering	Selbstversorger	zelbstferzorger
self-employed	freiberuflich	fryberooflikh
self-service	die Selbstbedienung	zelbstbedeenoong
to sell	verkaufen	ferkowfen
do you sell...?	verkaufen Sie...?	ferkowfen zee...?
to send	schicken	shikken

English	German	Pronunciation
separated (couple)	getrennt	getrent
serious	schlimm	shlim
service (in shop, etc)	die Bedienung	bedee-noong
is service included?	ist die Bedienung inbegriffen?	ist dee bedeenoong inbegriffen?
set menu	die Tageskarte	tahges-kar-te
several	verschiedene	fershee-de-ne
shallow (water)	seicht	zykht
to share	teilen	tylen
sharp	scharf	sharf
shaver	der Rasierapparat	razeer-apa-raht
she	sie	zee
sheltered	geschützt	geshuetst
to shine	scheinen	shynen
ship	das Schiff	shif
shirt	das Hemd	hemt

English – German

English – German

English	German	Pronunciation
shoe	der Schuh	shoo
shoe shop	der Schuhladen	**shoo**lahden
shop	der Laden	**lah**den
to shop	einkaufen	**yn**-kowfen
shop assistant	der Verkäufer/ die Verkäuferin	fer**koyf**er/ fer**koyf**er-rin
shopping	der Einkauf	**yn**-kowf
shopping centre	das Einkaufs- zentrum	**yn**-kowfs- **tsent**r<u>oo</u>m
short	kurz	koorts
short-sighted	kurzsichtig	**koorts**-zikhtikh
to shout	rufen	**roo**fen
to show	zeigen	**tsy**gen
shower (bath)	die Dusche	**doo**-she
(of rain)	der Schauer	**show**er
to shrink	einlaufen	**yn**-lowfen
shut (closed)	geschlossen	ge**shloss**en
to shut	schließen	**shlee**-sen
sick (ill)	krank	krank
(nauseous)	übel	**ueb**el
I feel sick	mir ist schlecht	meer ist shlekht
side	die Seite	**zy**-te
sidewalk	der Bürgersteig	**buer**gershtyg
sight	die Sehens- würdigkeit	**zeh**ens-vuer- dikh-kyt
sightseeing tour	die Besichti- gungstour	be-**zikh**ti- g<u>oo</u>ngs-too-er
to sign	unterschreiben	<u>oo</u>nter**shry**ben
signature	die Unterschrift	**oo**ntershrift
to sing	singen	**zing**-en
single (unmarried)	ledig	**leh**dikh
single (not double) (ticket)	Einzel- einfach	**yn**-tsel **yn**-fakh
single bed	das Einzelbett	**yn**-tsel-bet
single room	das Einzelzimmer	**yn**-tsel-tsimmer
sister	die Schwester	**shves**ter
sister-in-law	die Schwägerin	**shveh**ger-rin
to sit	sitzen	**zits**en
size (clothes, etc)	die Größe	**grur'**-se
to skate (on ice)	Schlittschuh laufen	**shlit**-shoo **low**fen
to ski	Ski fahren	**shee**fahren

English	German	
skiing	das Skilaufen	shee-lowfen
skin	die Haut	howt
skirt	der Rock	rok
to sleep	schlafen	shlahfen
sleeper (on train)	der Schlafwagen	shlahf-vahgen
to slip	rutschen	root-shen
slippers	die Hausschuhe	hows-shoo-e
slow(ly)	langsam	langzam
to slow down	langsamer werden	langzamer vehrden
small	klein	klyn
smaller than	kleiner als	klyner als
smell	der Geruch	gerookh
(unpleasant)	der Gestank	geshtank
to smell	riechen	ree-khen
to smile	lächeln	le-kheln
smoke	der Rauch	rowkh
to smoke	rauchen	row-khen
I don't smoke	ich bin Nichtraucher(in)	ikh bin nikht-row-kher(-rin)
smooth	weich	vykh

English	German	
to sneeze	niesen	neezen
snow	der Schnee	shnay
to snow: it's snowing	es schneit	es shnyt
soap	die Seife	zy-fe
socks	die Socken	zokken
soda water	Soda	sohdah
soft	weich	vykh
soft drink	alkoholfreies Getränk	alko-hohlfry-es getrenk
some	einige	y-ni-ge
someone	irgendjemand	irgent-yeh-mant
something	etwas	etvas
son	der Sohn	zohn
son-in-law	der Schwiegersohn	shveeger-zohn
soon	bald	balt
as soon as possible	so bald wie möglich	zoh balt vee murg'likh
sorry: I'm sorry!	tut mir leid!	toot meer lyt!

English – German

English	German	pronunciation
sort	die Sorte	**zor**-te
what sort?	welche Sorte?	**vel**-khe **zor**-te?
soup	die Suppe	**zoop**-e
sour	sauer	**zow**-er
soured cream	die saure Sahne	**zow**-re **zah**-ne
south	der Süden	**zue**den
spa	das Bad	baht
space	der Platz	plats
Spain	Spanien	**shpah**ni-en
Spanish (adj)	spanisch	**shpah**nish
sparkling	perlent	**perl**ent
sparkling water	das Sprudelwasser; der Sprudel	**shprood**el-vasser; **shproo**del
sparkling wine	der Schaumwein; der Sekt	**showm**vyn; zekt
to speak	sprechen	**shprekh**-en
do you speak English?	sprechen Sie Englisch?	**shprekh**-en zee **eng**-lish?
special	speziell	shpetsi-**el**
speciality	die Spezialität	shpetsi-ali-**teht**
speed limit	die Geschwindigkeitsbegrenzung	ge-**shvin**dikh-kyts-be-**grent**soong
to spell: *how is it spelt?*	wie buchstabiert man das?	vee bookh-shta-**beert** man das?
to spend	ausgeben	**ows**gehben
spicy	würzig	**vuert**sikh
to spill	verschütten	fer**shuett**en
spoilt	verdorben	fer**dor**ben
spoon	der Löffel	**lur'f**-el
sports centre	das Fitnesscenter	**fit**-nes-senter
sports shop	das Sportgeschäft	**shport**-gesheft
sprain	die Verstauchung	fer-**shtow**khoong
spring (season)	der Frühling	**frue**-ling
square (in town)	der Platz	plats
staff	das Personal	per-zo-**nahl**
stain	der Fleck	flek
stairs	die Treppe	**trep**-e
stale (bread)	trocken	**trokk**en

English	German	Pronunciation
stamp	die Briefmarke	**breef**mar-ke
to stand	stehen	**shteh**-en
to start (begin)	anfangen	**anfang**-en
starter (in meal)	die Vorspeise	**for**shpy-ze
station	der Bahnhof	**bahn**-hohf
stationer's	die Schreibwarenhandlung	**shryb**-vahren- hant-loong
to stay (remain)	bleiben	**blyb**en
to steal	stehlen	**shtehl**en
steamed	gedünstet	ge**duen**stet
steep	steil	shtyl
stereo	die Stereoanlage	**shteh**-reh-oh- **an**-lah-ge
to stick (with glue)	kleben	**kleh**ben
still (yet)	noch	nokh
still water	stilles Wasser	**shtilles vasser**
to sting	stechen	**shtekh**-en
stolen	gestohlen	ge**shtoh**-len
stomach ache	die Magenschmerzen	**mahgen**-shmertsen
to stop	halten	**halt**en
storm	der Sturm	shtoorm
story	die Geschichte	ge**shikh**-te
straight on	geradeaus	gerah-de-**ows**
strange (odd)	seltsam	**zelt**sam
straw (drinking)	der Strohhalm	**shtroh**-halm
street	die Straße	**shtrah**-se
striped	gestreift	ge**shtryft**
stroke	der Schlaganfall	**shlahg**-anfal
strong	stark	shtark
stuck: it's stuck	es klemmt	es klemmt
student discount	die Studentenermäßigung	shtoo**den**-ten-er- **meh**si-goong
stupid	dumm	doom
subtitles	die Untertitel	**oon**tertitel
sugar-free	zuckerfrei	**tsoo**kerfry
suitcase	der Koffer	**koffer**
summer	der Sommer	**zom**mer
summer holidays	die Sommerferien	**zom**mer- fehri-en
sun	die Sonne	**zon**-e
to sunbathe	sonnenbaden	**zon**nenbahden

English – German

English – German

sunblock	die Sonnencreme **zonn**enkrehm	sweater	der Pullover	pool-**ohv**er zues
sunburn	der Sonnenbrand **zonn**enbrant	sweet (not savoury)	süß	zues-shtof
Sunday	Sonntag **zon**-tahk	sweetener	der Süßstoff	zue**sikh**-kyten
sunglasses	die Sonnenbrille **zonn**enbrill-e	sweets	die Süßigkeiten	shvimmen
sunny	sonnig **zonn**ikh	to swim	schwimmen	bah**de-an**sook
sunrise	der **zonn**en-	swimming pool	das Schwimmbad **shvim**baht	
	Sonnenaufgang **ow**fgang **zonn**en-	swimsuit	der Badeanzug	**shvyt**-ser-rish
sunset	der Sonnen-	Swiss adj	schweizerisch	**ows**-shalten
	untergang **oon**tergang **zonn**en-shirm	to switch off (light)	ausschalten	
sunshade	der Sonnen- schirm	to switch on (light, machine)	abschalten	**ap**shalten
			abstellen	**ap**shtellen
supermarket	der Supermarkt **zoo**permarkt		einschalten	**yn**-shalten
supper	das Abendessen **ah**bent-essen	Switzerland		
supplement (to pay)	der Zuschlag **tsoo**shlahg	**T**		
sure: I'm sure	ich bin mir **kh bin meer** sicher **zikher**	to swim	anstellen	**an**shtellen
surname	der Nachname **nahkh**-nah-me		die Schweiz	shvyts
surprise	die Überraschung ueber-**rash**oong	table	der Tisch	tish
to survive	überleben ueber**leh**ben	table tennis	Tischtennis	**tish**tennis
to sweat	schwitzen **shvits**en			

table wine	der Tafelwein	tah-felvyn
to take	nehmen	nehmen
how long does it take?	wie lange dauert es?	vee lang-e dowert es?
take-away food	Essen zum Mitnehmen	essen tsoom mitnehmen
to take off	abfliegen	apfleegen
to talk to	sprechen mit	shprekhen mit
tall	groß	grohs
to taste	probieren	probeer-ren
tax	die Steuer	shtoyer
tea	der Tee	teh
herbal tea	der Kräutertee	kroyterteh
tea bag	der Teebeutel	tehboytel
teapot	die Teekanne	tehkan-e
to teach	unterrichten	oonter-rikhten
teacher	der Lehrer/die Lehrerin	lehrer/lehrer-rin
teeth	die Zähne	tseh-ne
telephone	das Telefon	telefohn
television	das Fernsehen	fern-zeh-en

to tell	erzählen	er-tsehlen
temperature	die Temperatur	temperatoor
temporary	provisorisch	provisoh-rish
tennis	Tennis	tennis
terminal	das Terminal	terminel
terrace	die Terrasse	te-ras-e
to test	testen	testen
text message	die SMS	es-em-es
to text	eine SMS schreiben	yn-e es-em-es shryben
than	als	als
to thank	danken	dangken
thank you	danke	dang-ke
thanks very much	vielen Dank	feelen dank
that	das	das
that one	das da	das dah
the	der, die, das	dehr, dee, das
theatre	das Theater	teh-ah-ter
their	ihr/ihre	eer/eer-re
them	ihnen	eenen

English – German

English	German	Pronunciation
there (over there)	dort	dort
there is	es gibt	es gipt
these	diese	dee-ze
they	sie	zee
thick (not thin)	dick	dik
thief	der Dieb	deep
thin	dünn	duen
thing	das Ding	ding
my things	meine Sachen	myn-e zakh-en
to think	denken	dengken
thirsty	durstig	doorstikh
to be thirsty	Durst haben	doorst hahben
this	dies	dees
this one	dieses hier	deezes heer
those	jene	yeh-ne
those ones	die dort	dee dort
throat lozenges	die Halspastillen	hals-pastillen
through	durch	doorkh
to throw away	wegwerfen	vek-verfen
thumb	der Daumen	dowmen
thunderstorm	das Gewitter	gevitter
Thursday	Donnerstag	donners-tahk
ticket (train, bus, etc)	die Karte	kar-te
(entrance fee)	die Eintrittskarte	yntrits-kar-te
ticket office	der Fahrkartenschalter	fahrkarten-shalter
tidy	ordentlich	ordentlikh
to tidy up	aufräumen	owf-roymen
tight	eng	eng
till (cash desk)	die Kasse	kas-e
till (until)	bis	bis
time (of day)	die Zeit	tsyt
what time is it?	wie spät ist es?	vee shpeht ist es?
timetable	der Fahrplan	fahrplan
to tip	Trinkgeld geben	trink-gelt gehben
tip (to waiter, etc)	das Trinkgeld	trink-gelt
tired	müde	muede
tissues	die Papiertaschentücher	papeer-tashen-tue-kher

to	zu (zum/zur)	tsoo (tsoom/ tsoor)
(with names of places)	nach	nahkh
today	heute	**hoy**-te
toe	die Zehe	**tseh**-e
together	zusammen	tsoo**zammen**
tomato juice	der Tomatensaft	to**mahten**-zaft
tomorrow	morgen	**morgen**
tonic water	das Tonic	**tonik**
tonight	heute Abend	hoyte **ah**bent
too (also)	auch	owkh
toothache	die Zahnschmerzen	**tsahn**-shmertsen
toothpick	der Zahnstocher	**tsahn**-shtokh-er
total (amount)	die Endsumme	ent**zoom**-e
to touch	anfassen	**an**fassen
tough (meat)	zäh	tseh
tour	die Fahrt	fahrt
guided tour	die Führung	**fuer**-roong

tour guide	der Reiseführer/ die Reiseführerin	**ry**-ze-fuer-rer/ **ry**-ze-fuer-rer-rin
tour operator	der Reiseveranstalter	**ry**-ze-fer-anshtalter
tourist office	das Fremdenverkehrsbüro	**fremden**-ferkehrs-bue-roh
towel	das Handtuch	**hant**-tookh
town	die Stadt	shtat
town centre	das Stadtzentrum	**shtat**-tsentroom
town hall	das Rathaus	**raht**-hows
traffic	der Verkehr	fer**kehr**
traffic jam	der Stau	shtow
traffic lights	die Ampel	**ampel**
train	der Zug	tsook
by train	mit dem Zug	mit dehm tsook
tram	die Straßenbahn	**shtrah**-sen-bahn
to translate	übersetzen	ueber**zetsen**

English – German

to travel	reisen	ryzen
travel agent's	das Reisebüro	ry-ze-bue-roh
travel sickness	die Reisekrankheit	ry-ze-krank-hyt
travellers' cheques	die Reiseschecks	ry-ze-sheks
tree	der Baum	bowm
trip	der Ausflug	owsflook
trolley (luggage)	der Gepäckwagen	gepekvahgen
trousers	die Hose	hoh-ze
true	wahr	vahr
to try	versuchen	ferzookhen
to try on	anprobieren	anprobeer-ren
Tuesday	Dienstag	deens-tahk
to turn (right/left)	abbiegen	apbeegen
to turn around	umdrehen	oomdreh-en
to turn off (light)	ausmachen	owsmakh-en
(TV, radio, etc)	ausschalten	ows-shalten
(tap)	zudrehen	tsoo-dreh-en
to turn on (light)	anmachen	anmakh-en
(TV, radio, etc)	anschalten	anshalten
(tap)	aufdrehen	owf-dreh-en
twice	zweimal	tsvymahl
twin-bedded room	Zweibettzimmer	tsvybet-tsimmer
typical	typisch	tuepish
Tyrol	Tirol	tirohl
U		
ugly	hässlich	hesslikh
uncle	der Onkel	ongkel
uncomfortable	unbequem	oon-be-kvehm
under	unter	oonter
undercooked	nicht gar	nikht gahr
underground	die U-Bahn	oobahn
understand	verstehen	fershteh-en
I don't understand	ich verstehe nicht	ikh fershteh-e nikht
unemployed	arbeitslos	arbytslohs
to unfasten	aufmachen	owfmakh-en

English	German	Pronunciation
United Kingdom	das Vereinigte Königreich	das fer-**ynik**-te **kur'**nig-rykh
United States	die Vereinigten Staaten	fer-**ynik**-ten **shtah**ten
university	die Universität	ooniverzi**teht**
unleaded petrol	das bleifreie Benzin	**bly**fry-e bent**seen**
unlikely	unwahrscheinlich	**oon**vahrshynlikh
to unlock	aufschließen	**owf**shlee-sen
to unpack	auspacken	**ows**pakken
unpleasant	unangenehm	**oon**an-genehm
until	bis	bis
up: *to get up*	aufstehen	**owf**shteh-en
upside down	verkehrt herum	fer**kehrt** her-**room**
upstairs	oben	**oh**ben
urgent	dringend	**dring**-ent
us	uns	oons
to use	benutzen	be**noot**-sen
useful	nützlich	**nuets**likh
username	der Benutzername	be**noot**ser-nah-me
usual(ly)	gewöhnlich	ge**vur'n**likh

V

English	German	Pronunciation
vacancy (hotel)	Zimmer frei	**tsimm**er fry
vacant	frei	fry
vacation	Urlaub	**oor**lowb
valid	gültig	**guel**tikh
valuable	wertvoll	**vehrt**fol
valuables	die Wertsachen	**vehrt**zakh-en
VAT	die Mehrwertsteuer (MWST)	**mehr**vehrt-shtoyer
vegan: *I'm vegan*	ich bin Veganer	ikh bin ve**gah**ner
vegetarian adj	vegetarisch	ve-ge-**tahr**ish
I'm vegetarian	ich bin Vegetarier	ikh bin ve-ge-**tahr**i-er
vehicle	das Fahrzeug	**fahr**-tsoyk
very	sehr	zehr
vet	der Tierarzt	**teer**artst

English – German

via	über	*ueber*
video game	das Videospiel	*veedh-oh-shpeel*
Vienna	Wien	*veen*
view	die Aussicht	*ows-zikht*
village	das Dorf	*dorf*
visa	das Visum	*veezoom*
visit	der Besuch	*besookh*
to visit (person)	besuchen	*besookh-en*
to visit (place)	besichtigen	*be-zikhti-gen*
voucher	der Gutschein	*goot-shyn*

W

to wait for	warten auf	*varten owf*
waiter/	der Kellner/	*kelner/*
waitress	die Kellnerin	*kelner-rin*
waiting room	der Warteraum	*var-te-rowm*
to wake up	aufwachen	*owfvakh-en*
Wales	Wales	*vels*
walk	der Spaziergang	*shpat-seergang*

to go for a walk	einen Spaziergang machen	*yn-en shpat-seergang makh-en*
	spazieren gehen	*shpat-seer-ren geh-en*
to walk		
(go on foot)	zu Fuß gehen	*tsoo foos geh-en*
wallet	die Brieftasche	*breef-tash-e*
to want	wollen	*vollen*
I want...	ich möchte...	*ikh mur'kh-te...*
we want...	wir möchten...	*veer mur'khten...*
war	der Krieg	*kreek*
warm	warm	*varm*
to warm up (milk, etc)	aufwärmen	*owfvermen*
to wash	waschen	*vashen*
wash and blow dry	waschen und föhnen	*vashen oont fur'nen*
wasp sting	der Wespenstich	*vespen-shtikh*
to watch	zuschauen	*tsooshowen*
water	die Armbanduhr	*armbant-oo-er*
	das Wasser	*vasser*

English	German	
waterproof	wasserdicht	**vasser**dikht
to water ski	Wasserski	**vasser**shee
	fahren	**fahren**
we	wir	veer
weak	schwach	shvakh
(tea, coffee)	dünn	dụen
to wear	tragen	**trah**gen
weather	das Wetter	**vetter**
weather	die Wettervor-	**vetter-**
forecast	hersage	for**hehr**zah-ge
wedding	der Hochzeitstag	**hokh**-tsyts-tahk
anniversary		
Wednesday	Mittwoch	**mit**-vokh
week	die Woche	**vokh**-e
weekend	das Wochenende	**vokh**en-en-de
weight	das Gewicht	ge**vikht**
welcome	willkommen	vil**kommen**
well	gut	goot
he's not well	ihm geht es	eem geht es
	nicht gut	nikht goot
well-done (steak)	durch	dọọrkh

English	German	
Welsh adj	walisisch	va**lee**zish
west	der Westen	**vesten**
wet	nass	nas
what	was	vas
when	wann	van
where	wo	voh
which	welcher/	**vel**-kher/
	welche/	**vel**-khe/
	welches	**vel**-khes
while	während	**veh**rent
in a while	bald	balt
white	weiß	vys
who	wer	vehr
wholemeal	Vollkornbrot	**fol**kornbroht
bread		
whose	wessen	**vess**en
why	warum	va-**room**
wide	breit	bryt
wife	die Frau	frow
to win	gewinnen	ge**vinnen**
wind	der Wind	vint

English – German

English - German

window	das Fenster	**fenster**
windy	windig	**vin**dikh
wine	der Wein	vyn
wine list	die Weinkarte	**vyn**-kar-te
winter	der Winter	**vin**ter
with	mit	mit
without	ohne	**oh**-ne
to withdraw cash	Geld abheben	gehlt ap**heh**ben
woman	die Frau	frow
wonderful	wunderbar	**voon**derbahr
wooden	hölzern	**hur'lts**ern
work	die Arbeit	**ahr**byt
to work (person)	arbeiten	**ahr**byten
(machine)	funktionieren	foonk-tsio-**neer**-ren
worried	besorgt	be**zorkt**
worse	schlechter	**shlehkh**ter
worth: *it's worth £50*	es ist fünfzig Pfund wert	es ist **fuenf**-tsikh pfoont vehrt
to write	schreiben	**shry**ben

wrong	falsch	falsh
what's wrong?	was stimmt nicht?	vas shtimt nikht?
X		
to X-ray	röntgen	**rur'nt**gen
Y		
year	das Jahr	yahr
this year	dieses Jahr	**dee**zes yahr
next year	nächstes Jahr	**neh**-kstes yahr
last year	letztes Jahr	**lets**-tes yahr
yearly	jährlich	**yehr**likh
yellow	gelb	gelp
Yellow Pages	die Gelben Seiten	gelben **zy**ten
yes	ja	yah
yesterday	gestern	**ges**tern
yet: *not yet*	noch nicht	nokh nikht
yoghurt	der Jogurt	**yoh**goort

plain yoghurt	der Naturjogurt	na**toor**-**yoh**g<u>oo</u>rt
you (formal sing. and pl.)	Sie	zee
(informal sing.)	du	doo
(pl.)	ihr	eer
young	jung	yoong
your	dein/deine	dyn/**dyn**-e
	Ihr/Ihre	eer/**eer**-re
youth hostel	die Jugendherberge	**yoog**ent-her-ber-ge
Z		
zero	null	n<u>oo</u>l

German - English

German	English
A	
ab	off, from
ab 8 Uhr	from 8 o'clock
ab Mai	from May onward
abbestellen	to cancel
abbiegen	to turn (right/left)
Abend m	evening
Abendessen nt	evening meal
abends	in the evening(s)
aber	but
abfahren	to depart; to leave
Abfahrt f	departures
Abfahrtszeit f	departure time
Abfertigungs-schalter m	check-in desk
abfliegen	to take off
Abflug m	flight departures
Abflugzeit f	departure time

German	English
abholen	to fetch; to claim (baggage, etc)
abholen lassen	to send for
ablaufen	to expire
Abreise f	departure
absagen	to cancel
abschalten	to switch off (machine)
Absender m	sender
abstellen	to turn off; to park car
Abteilung f	department
achten auf	to pay attention to
Achtung f	caution; danger
ähnlich	similar
Aktentasche f	briefcase
akzeptieren	to accept
alkoholfrei	non-alcoholic
alkoholisch	alcoholic (drink)

German	English
alle	all; everybody; everyone
alle zwei Tage	every other day
allein	alone
allergisch	gegen allergic to
alles	everything; all
allgemein	general; universal
alt	old
Altbier nt	top-fermented dark beer
Alter nt	age (of person)
ältere(r/s)	older; elder
am	at; in; on
am Bahnhof	at the station
am Abend	in the evening
am Freitag	on Friday
Amerika nt	America
amerikanisch adj	American
Ampel f	traffic light

German	English
an	at; on (light, radio, etc); near
an/aus	on/off
Ananas f	pineapple
anbieten	to offer
andere(r/s)	other
ändern	to change (to alter)
Anfang m	start (beginning)
anfangen	to begin; to start
Anfrage f	enquiry
Angebot m	offer
im Angebot	on offer
angenehm	pleasant
ankommen	to arrive
ankündigen	to announce
Ankunft f	arrivals
Anmelde-formular nt	registration form
Anmeldung f	reception (place)
annehmen	to assume; to accept
anprobieren	to try on
Anruf m	phone call
Anrufbeant-worter m	answerphone
anrufen	to phone
anschalten	to turn on
anschauen	to look at
Anschluss m	connection (train, etc)
anschnallen	to fasten
Ansicht f	view
Ansichtskarte f	picture postcard
anstatt	instead of
ansteckend	infectious
anstehen	to queue
anstellen	to switch on (gas, etc)
Antwort f	answer; reply
antworten	to answer; to reply
Anweisungen pl	instructions
Apfel (Äpfel) m	apple(s)
Apfelsaft m	apple juice
Apfelsine(n) f	orange(s)
Apfelwein m	cider
Apotheke f	pharmacy
Aprikose(n) f	apricot(s)
April m	April
Arbeit f	employment; work
arbeiten	to work (person)
arbeitslos	unemployed
arm	poor
Arm m	arm
Armbanduhr f	watch
Art f	type; sort; manner
Arzt (Ärztin) m/f	doctor
atmen	to breathe

German – English

German	English
auch	also; too; as well
auf	onto; on; upon; on top of
auf Deutsch	in German
auf Wiedersehen	goodbye
aufdrehen	to turn on (tap)
Aufenthalt *m*	stay; visit
Aufenthalts-raum *m*	lounge
Auffahrt *f*	slip-road; driveway
aufhalten	to delay; to hold up
sich aufhalten	to stay
aufmachen	to open (*shop, bank etc*); to unfasten
aufregend	exciting
aufschließen	to unlock
aufschreiben	to write down
aufstehen	to get up
aufwachen	to wake up
Aufzug *m*	lift/elevator
Augenblick *m*	moment; instant
August *m*	August
aus	off (*light, radio, etc*); made of...; from; out of
Ausdruck *m*	expression
Ausfahrt *f*	exit (*motorway*)
Ausfall *m*	failure (*mechanical*)
Ausflug *m* (-flüge)	trip(s); excursion(s)
ausfüllen	to fill in (*form*)
Ausgaben *pl*	expenses
Ausgang *m*	exit; gate (*at airport*)
ausgeben	to spend (*money*)
ausgehen	to go out (*for amusement*)
ausgezeichnet	excellent
Auskunft *f*	information
aus dem Ausland	from overseas
Ausländer(in) *m/f*	foreigner
Ausnahme *f*	exception
auspacken	to unpack
ausschalten	to switch off (*light, TV, radio*)
außer Betrieb	out of order
Aussicht *f*	view; prospect
aussprechen	to pronounce
Ausstellungs-datum *nt*	date of issue
Australien *nt*	Australia
australisch *adj*	Australian
Ausverkauf *m*	sale
ausverkauft	sold out
Auswahl *f*	choice
Auto(s) *nt*	car(s)
Autobahn *f*	motorway

German	English
Autobahngebühr f	toll
Autokarte f	road map
Automat wechselt	change given
automatisch	automatic
Autovermietung f	car hire

B

German	English
Bäckerei f	baker's
Bad nt	bath; spa
Badeanzug m	swimsuit
Badehose f	swimming trunks
baden	to bathe; to swim
Baden verboten	no swimming
Badezimmer nt	bathroom
Bahn f	railway; rink
Bahnhof m	station; depot
Bahnsteig m	platform
Bahnübergang m	level crossing
bald	soon
Banane(n) f	banana(s)
Bankkonto nt	bank account
Bargeld nt	cash
Basel	Basle
bauen	to build
Bauer (Bäuerin) m/f	farmer
Bauernmarkt m	farmers' market
Baum m	tree
Baumwolle f	cotton (fabric)
Baustelle f	roadworks; construction site
Bayern nt	Bavaria
beachten	to observe; to obey
beantworten	to answer
Bedarfshaltestelle f	request stop
bedeckt	cloudy (weather)
Bedeutung f	meaning
bedienen	to operate
sich bedienen	to help oneself
Bedienung f	service charge; waiter/waitress
Bedingung f	condition
beenden	to end; to finish
Beere f	berry
beginnen	to begin
behalten	to keep (retain)
Behandlung f	treatment
beheizt	heated
behindert	disabled (person)
bei	near; by (beside); at; on; during
beide	both
Beilage f	side-dish
Beispiel(e) nt	example(s)

German – English

German	English
Bekleidungsgeschäft nt	clothes shop
bekommen	to get (receive, obtain)
belegt	no vacancies
beliebt	popular
benachrichtigen	to inform
benötigen	to require
benutzen	to use
Benzin nt	petrol
bequem	comfortable
berechtigt zu	entitled to
bereit	ready
Berg(e) m	mountain(s)
Bericht(e) m	report(s); bulletin(s)
Berliner m	doughnut
Beruf m	profession; occupation
berühmt	famous
berühren	to touch

German	English
beschädigen	to damage
beschäftigt	busy
beschreiben	to describe
Beschreibung f	description
Beschwerde f	complaint
besetzt	engaged; occupied
besichtigen	to visit (place)
Besichtigungen pl	sightseeing
Besichtigungstour f	guided tour
besondere(r/s)	particular; special
besorgt	worried
besser	better
gute Besserung	get well soon
bestätigen	to confirm
Bestätigung f	confirmation (flight, etc)
beste(r/s)	best

German	English
bestellen	to book; to order
besuchen	to visit (person)
Besucher(in) m/f	visitor
Betrag m	amount
Betrag erhalten	payment received
betreten	to enter
Bettdecke f	duvet; quilt
Bettzeug nt	bedclothes
bewölkt	cloudy
bezahlen	to pay; to settle bill
Bezahlung f	payment
Bienenstich m	bee sting; type of cream cake
Bier vom Fass nt	draught beer
Bierstube f	pub that specializes in beer
bieten	to offer

German	English
billig	cheap; inexpensive
Billigtarif m	cheap rate
Birne(n) f	pear(s)
bis	until; till
bis jetzt	up till now
bis bald	see you soon
bisschen:	
ein bisschen	a little; a bit of
bitte	please
bitte?	pardon?
blass	pale
blau	blue
bleiben	to stay *(to remain)*
bleifreies Benzin nt	unleaded petrol
Blitz m	lightning
blockiert	jammed *(camera, lock)*
Blockschrift f	block letters

German	English
Blumen pl	flowers
Blutdruck m	blood pressure
bluten	to bleed
Blutgruppe f	blood group
blutig	rare *(steak)*
Bockbier nt	strong beer
Bodensee m	Lake Constance
Bohnen pl	beans
Bootsfahrt f	cruise
Bootsverleih m	boat hire
Bordkarte f	boarding pass
Botschaft f	embassy
braten	to fry; to roast
Bratkartoffeln pl	fried potatoes
Bratwurst f	sausage
brauchen	to need
Brauerei f	brewery
braun	brown
breit	wide
Briefkasten m	letterbox; postbox

German	English
Briefmarke(n) f	stamp(s)
Briefpapier nt	writing paper
Brieftasche f	wallet
Briefumschlag m	envelope
Brille f	glasses *(spectacles)*
bringen	to bring
britisch	British
Brot nt	bread; loaf
Brötchen nt	bread roll
Brücke f	bridge
Buch(Bücher) m	book
Buch nt	book
buchen	to book
Buchhandlung f	bookshop
Buchung f	booking
bügeln	to iron
bunt	coloured
Burg f	castle; fortress *(medieval)*

German – English

Bürgersteig *m*	pavement; sidewalk	**Dampfer** *m*	steamer (boat)
Büro *nt*	agency; office	**danach**	after (afterwards)
Busbahnhof *m*	bus/coach station	**Dänemark** *nt*	Denmark
Bushaltestelle *f*	bus stop	**danke**	thank you
Busreise *f*	coach trip	**danken**	to thank
		das	the; that; this; which
C		**Datum** *nt*	date (day)
Campingplatz *m*	campsite	**Dauer** *f*	length; duration
Champignon(s) *m f*	mushroom(s)	**Decke** *f*	blanket; ceiling
Chef(in) *m f*	boss	**dein**	your (informal singular)
Chips *pl*	crisps	**denken**	to think
Chor *m*	choir	**Denkmal-** **(-mäler)** *nt*	monument(s)
Computerspiel *nt*	computer game	**Deo** *nt*	deodorant
		der	the; who(m); that; this; which
D		**deutsch** *adj*	German
da	there		
nicht da	out (not at home)		
daheim	at home		
Damen	ladies		

Deutsch *nt*	German (language)		
Deutsche(r) *m f*	German		
Devisen *pl*	foreign currency		
Dezember *m*	December		
Dia(s) *nt*	slide(s)		
dick	fat		
die	the; who(m); that; this; which		
Diebstahl *m*	theft		
Dienst *m*	service		
im Dienst	on duty		
Dienstag *m*	Tuesday		
dienstbereit	open (pharmacy); on duty (doctor)		
Dienstreise *f*	business trip		
Dienstzeit *f*	office hours		
dies	this		
diese	these		
diese(r/s)	this (one)		
Ding(e) *nt*	thing(s)		

German	English
Direktflug m	direct flight
Dom m	cathedral
Donner m	thunder
Donnerstag m	Thursday
Doppel-	double
Doppelbett nt	double bed
doppelt	double
Doppelzimmer nt	double room
Dorf (Dörfer) nt	village(s)
dort	there (over there); that one
Dozent(in) m/f	teacher (university)
draußen	outdoors; outside
drehen	to turn; to twist
Dreibettabteil nt	three-berth compartment
dringend	urgent
drinnen	indoors
Droge f	drug
Drogerie f	chemist's (not for prescriptions)
drücken	push
Druckschrift f	block letters
du	you (informal singular)
dumm	stupid
dunkel	dark
dunkelblau	dark blue
dünn	thin; weak (tea)
dunstig	misty
durch	through; well-done (steak)
Durchfahrt verboten	no through traffic
Durchfall m	diarrhoea
Durchgangsverkehr m	through traffic
durchgehend	direct (train, bus); 24 hour
Durchzug m	draught (of air)
dürfen	to be allowed
Dürre f	drought
durstig	thirsty
Dusche f	shower
Dutzend nt	dozen

E

German	English
echt	real; genuine
Ecke f	corner
ehemalig	ex-
ehrlich	honest
Ei(er) nt	egg(s)
eifersüchtig	jealous
Eigelb nt	egg yolk
Eilbrief m	express letter
Eilzustellung f	special delivery
ein	(with 'das'/'der' words) a; one
ein(geschaltet)	on (machine)
Einbahnstraße f	one-way street
einchecken	to check in

German – English

German - English

German	English
eine	(with 'die' words) a; one
einfach	simple; single ticket; plain (unflavoured)
Eingang m	entrance
Eingangstür f	front door
eingeschlossen	included (in price)
einige(r/s)	some; a few
einkaufen	to shop
Einkaufszentrum nt	shopping centre
einladen	to invite
Einladung f	invitation
Einlass ab 18	no entry for under-18s
einlösen	to cash (cheque)
einmal	once
einnehmen	to take (medicine)
einschalten	to switch on (light, TV)
einschließlich	including
einsteigen	to get in(to) (bus, etc)
Einstellplatz m	car port
Eintopfgericht nt	stew
Eintritt frei	free entry
Eintrittspreis m	admission charge/fee
Einwurf 2 Euro	insert 2 euros
Einzahlung f	deposit
Einzelfahrschein m	single ticket
einzeln	single; individual
Einzelzimmer nt	single room
Eis nt	ice cream; ice
Eisbecher m	knickerbocker glory
Eisdiele f	ice-cream parlour
Eiskaffee m	iced coffee
Eistee m	iced tea
Eiswürfel pl	ice cubes
Eiweiß nt	egg white
Elektrorasierer m	electric razor
Ellbogen m	elbow
Eltern pl	parents
Empfang m	reception
Empfangsschein m	receipt
empfehlen	to recommend
Endstation f	terminal
Endsumme f	total (amount)
eng	narrow; tight (clothes)
England nt	England
Engländer(in) m/f	Englishman/woman
Englisch nt	English (language)
Enkel m	grandson
Enkelin f	granddaughter
Ente f	duck

German	English
enteisen	to de-ice
entfernt	away
2 Kilometer entfernt	2 km away
entfrosten	to defrost
entrahmte Milch *f*	skimmed milk
entschädigen	to reimburse
Entschuldigung *f*	pardon; excuse me
entweder ... oder	either ... or
entwickeln	to develop (photos)
Entzündung *f*	inflammation
epileptischer Anfall *m*	epileptic fit
er	he; it
Erbsen *pl*	peas
Erdbeeren *pl*	strawberries
Erdgeschoss *nt*	ground floor
Erdnuss(-nüsse) *f*	peanut(s)
erfreut	pleased
Erfrischungen *pl*	refreshments
erhalten	to obtain; to receive
erhältlich	available
Erkältung *f*	cold (illness)
erkennen	to realize; to recognize
erklären	to explain
Erklärung *f*	explanation
erlauben	to permit (something); to allow
Ermäßigung *f*	reduction
Ersatz *m*	substitute; replacement
erste(r/s)	first
erste Hilfe	first aid
Erwachsene(r) *m/f*	adult
erzählen	to tell
es	it
essbar	edible
essen	to eat
Essen *nt*	food; meal
Essen zum Mitnehmen	take-away food
Essig *m*	vinegar
Esslöffel *m*	tablespoon
Esszimmer *nt*	dining room
Etage *f*	floor; storey
Etagenbetten *pl*	bunk beds
etwas	something
europäisch	European
Exemplar *nt*	copy
Experte (Expertin *f*) *m/f*	expert

F

German	English
Fabrik *f*	works; factory
Facharzt (Fachärztin *f*) *m/f*	specialist (medical)
Fahrbahn *f*	carriageway

German – English

German	English
Fähre f	ferry
fahren	to drive; to go
Fahrer(in) m/f	driver (of car)
Fahrgast m	passenger
Fahrkarte f	ticket (train, bus, etc)
Fahrkartenschalter m	ticket office
Fahrplan m	timetable (trains, etc)
Fahrplanhinweise pl	travel information
Fahrrad(räder) nt	bicycle(s)
Fahrschein(e) m	ticket(s)
Fahrscheinentwerter m	ticket stamping machine
Fahrscheinheft nt	book of tickets
Fahrstuhl m	lift; elevator
Fahrt f	journey
gute Fahrt!	safe journey!
Fahrzeug nt	vehicle
Fall: im Falle von	in case of
fallen	to fall
falsch	false (name, etc); wrong
Familie f	family
Familienname m	surname
Familienstand m	marital status
Farbe f	colour
Farbfilm m	colour film
farbig	coloured
Fasching m	carnival
Fass nt	barrel
vom Fass	on tap; on draught
Fassbier nt	draught beer
faul	lazy
Februar m	February
fehlen	to be missing
Fehler m	fault; mistake
feiern	to celebrate
Feiertag m	holiday
Fenster nt	window
Ferien pl	holiday(s)
Ferngespräch nt	long-distance call
Fernsehen nt	television
fertig	ready; finished
Fest nt	celebration; party; festival
fettarme Milch f	low-fat milk
fettig	greasy
feuergefährlich	inflammable
Fieber nt	fever
Fieber haben	to have a temperature
Filzstift m	felt-tip pen
finden	to find
Firma f	company (firm)
Fisch m	fish
flach	flat (level); shallow (water)

German	English
Flasche f	bottle
Flaschenbier nt	bottled beer
Fleisch nt	meat; flesh
fliegen	to fly
Flöhe pl	fleas
Flug (Flüge) m	flight(s)
Fluggast m	passenger
Flughafen m	airport
Flughafenbus m	airport bus
Flugauskunft f	flight information
Flugschein(e) m	plane ticket(s)
Flugsteig m	gate
Flugzeug nt	plane, aircraft
Fluss (Flüsse) m	river(s)
folgen	to follow
Forelle f	trout
Fotoapparat m	camera
Fotogeschäft nt	photo shop
Frage f	question
fragen	to ask
frankieren	to stamp (letter)
Frankreich nt	France
Franzose (Französin) m/f	Frenchman/woman
französisch adj	French
Frau f	wife; Mrs; Ms; woman
Fräulein nt	Miss
frei	free/vacant
im Freien	outdoor
Freibad nt	open-air pool
freiberuflich	freelance; self-employed
Freigepäck nt	baggage allowance
Freiland	free-range
Freitag m	Friday
Freizeichen nt	dialling tone
Freizeit f	spare time; leisure
Freizeitzentrum nt	leisure centre
fremd	foreign; strange (unknown)
Freude f	joy
Freund m	friend; boyfriend
Freundin f	friend; girlfriend
freundlich	friendly
frisch	fresh; wet (paint)
Frischkäse m	cream cheese
Friseur (Friseuse) m/f	hairdresser
Früchte pl	fruit
Früchtetee m	fruit tea
Fruchtsaft m	fruit juice
früh	early
Frühling m	spring (season)
Frühstück nt	breakfast
fühlen	to feel
führen	to lead
Führerschein m	driving licence

German – English

German – English

German	English
füllen	to fill
Fundbüro *nt*	lost property office
für	for
Fuß (Füße) *m*	foot (feet)
zu Fuß gehen	to walk
Fußballspiel *nt*	football match
Fußgänger- überweg *m*	pedestrian crossing
Fußgängerzone *f*	pedestrian precinct

G

German	English
Gabel *f*	fork (for eating)
Gang *m*	course (of meal); aisle (theatre, plane)
Gans *f*	goose
ganz	whole; quite
ganztägig	full-time

German	English
Garantie *f*	guarantee; warrant(y)
Garten *m*	garden
Gartenlokal *nt*	garden café
Gasse *f*	alley; lane (in town)
Gast *m*	guest
Gasthaus *nt*	inn
Gasthof *m*	guesthouse
Gaststätte *f*	restaurant
Gaststube *f*	lounge; restaurant
Gebäck *nt*	pastry (cake)
gebacken	baked
gebeizt	cured; marinated
geben	to give
geboren	born
gebraten	fried
gebrauchen	to use
gebrochen	broken
Gebühr *f*	fee

German	English
gebührenpflichtig	subject to fee
Geburtsdatum *nt*	date of birth
Geburtsort *m*	place of birth
Geburtstag *m*	birthday
Gedeckpreis *m*	cover charge (in restaurant)
gedünstet	steamed
gefährlich	dangerous
gefroren	frozen (food)
gefüllt	stuffed
gegen	versus; against; toward(s)
Gegend *f*	district; region
gegenüber	opposite; facing
gegrillt	grilled
Geheimzahl *f*	PIN number
gehen	to go; to walk
gekocht	boiled; cooked
gelb	yellow
Gelbe Seiten *pl*	Yellow Pages
Geld *nt*	money

German	English
Geld abheben	withdraw cash
Geld einwerfen nt	insert money
Geldautomat m	cash dispenser; ATM
Geldbeutel m	purse
Geldrückgabe f	coin return
Geldstrafe f	fine (to be paid)
Geldstück nt	coin
gelegentlich	occasionally
Geltungsdauer f	period of validity
gemischt	mixed; assorted
Gemüse nt	vegetables
genau	accurate; precise; exact
genfrei	GM-free
genmanipuliert	genetically modified
genug	enough
geöffnet	open
Gepäck nt	luggage
Gepäckaufbe-wahrung f	left-luggage office
Gepäckausgabe f	baggage reclaim
geradeaus	straight ahead
geräuchert	smoked (food)
geröstet	sauté; fried; toasted
Gesamtsumme f	total amount
Geschäft(e) nt	business; shop(s)
Geschäfts-führer(in) m/f	manager
Geschäfts-stunden pl	business hours
geschehen	to happen
Geschenk(e) nt	gift(s)
Geschenke-laden m	gift shop
Geschichte f	history
geschieden	divorced
geschlossen	closed; shut
Geschmack m	taste; flavour
geschmort	braised
geschnittenes Brot nt	sliced bread
Geschoss nt	storey
geschützt	sheltered
Geschwindigkeit f	speed
Gesellschaft f	company
Gesetz nt	law
gesetzlicher Feiertag m	public holiday
Gesicht nt	face
gesperrt	closed
Gespräch nt	talk; phone call
Gesprächs-guthaben nt	credit (on mobile phone)
Gestank m	smell (unpleasant)
gestattet	permitted
gestern	yesterday

German - English

German	English
gestochen	stung; bitten (by insect)
gestreift	striped
gesund	healthy
Gesundheit f	health; bless you!
Getränk(e) nt	drink(s)
getrennt	separated (couple)
Gewicht nt	weight
gewinnen	to win
Gewitter nt	thunderstorm
gewöhnlich	usual(ly)
Gewürz nt	spice; seasoning
gibt es...?	is/are there...?
giftig	poisonous
Glas nt	glass; jar
Glatteis nt	black ice
glatzköpfig	bald (person)
glauben	to think (be of opinion)
gleich	same
Gleise pl	platforms; tracks
Glück nt	happiness; luck
glücklich	happy; lucky
glutenfrei	gluten-free
Grad m	degree (of heat, cold)
Gras nt	grass
Gräte f	fish bone
grau	grey
Grenze f	frontier; border (of country)
Grillstube f	steak house; grillroom
Grillteller m	mixed grill
Grippe f	flu
groß	tall; great; big; high (number, speed)
Großbritannien nt	Great Britain
Größe f	size (of clothes, shoes); height
Großeltern pl	grandparents
großzügig	generous
grün	green; fresh (fish)
grüner Salat m	green salad
Gruppe f	group
Gruß m	greeting
gültig	valid
günstig	convenient; cheap
Gurke(n) f	cucumber(s); gherkin(s)
Gürteltasche f	bumbag; moneybelt
gut	good; well; all right (yes)
guten Appetit	enjoy your meal
guten Tag	hello; good day/afternoon

German	English
Guthabenkarte *f*	charge card *(for mobile phone)*
Gutschein *m*	voucher; coupon

H

German	English
H-Milch *f*	long-life milk
Haare *pl*	hair
Haarschnitt *m*	haircut
haben	to have
Hackfleisch *nt*	mince meat
Hafen *m*	harbour; port
Hafer *m*	oats
Hähnchen *nt*	chicken
halb	half
halb durch	medium rare *(meat)*
Halbfettmilch *f*	semi-skimmed milk
Halbinsel *f*	peninsula
Halbpension *f*	half board
Hälfte *f*	half
Halspastillen *pl*	throat lozenges
Halsschmerzen *pl*	sore throat
Halt *m*	stop
Haltbarkeits- datum *nt*	sell-by date
halten	to hold; to stop
Halten verboten	no stopping
Haltestelle *f*	bus stop
Hand *f*	hand
handgemacht	handmade
Handgepäck *nt*	hand-luggage
Handtasche *f*	handbag
Handtuch *nt*	towel
Handy *nt*	mobile *(phone)*
Handynummer *f*	mobile number
hart gekochtes Ei *nt*	hard-boiled egg
hässlich	ugly
häufig	frequent; common
Hauptbahnhof *m*	main station
Hauptgericht *nt*	main course
Hauptstadt *f*	capital *(city)*
Haus *nt*	house; home
zu Hause	at home
Hauswein *m*	house wine
Heidel- beeren *pl*	blueberries
heilig	holy
Heiligabend *m*	Christmas Eve
heiraten	to marry
heiß	hot
heiße Schokolade *f*	hot chocolate
heißen	to be called
Heizung *f*	heating
helfen	to help
helles Bier *nt*	lager
Hemd(en) *nt*	shirt(s)
Herbst *m*	autumn
herein	in; come in
hereinkommen	to come in

German – English

German – English

German	English
Herr m	gentleman; Mr
heruntergehen	to go down
Herzanfall m	heart attack
herzliche Glückwünsche!	congratulations!
Heuschnupfen m	hay fever
heute	today
heute Abend	tonight
hier	here
hiesig	local (wine, speciality)
Hilfe f	help
Himbeeren pl	raspberries
Himmel m	heaven; sky
Hin- und Rückfahrt f	round trip
hineingehen	to go in
hinten; hinter	behind
hoch	high
Hochsaison f	high season

German	English
Höchstgeschwindigkeit f	maximum speed
Höchsttarif m	peak rate
hoffen	to hope
höflich	polite
hoher Blutdruck m	high blood pressure
höher	higher
holen	to fetch
holländisch	Dutch
Holz nt	wood (material)
homöopathisch	homeopathic
Honig m	honey
hören	to hear
Hörnchen nt	croissant
Hose f	trousers
Hotel garni nt	bed and breakfast hotel
hübsch	pretty
Hühnchen nt	chicken
Hummer m	lobster

German	English
Hund m	dog
Hunger haben	to be hungry
husten	to cough
Hustenbonbons pl	cough sweets
Hustensaft m	cough mixture
I	
ich	I
Idiotenhügel m	nursery slope
ihm	him
ihnen	them
ihr(e)	her; their
Imbiss m	snack
Imbissstube f	snack bar
immer	always
in Ordnung	all right (agreed)
Inland nt	domestic (flight, etc)
Inlandsgespräch(e) nt	national call(s)

German	English
innen	inside
Insektenschutz-mittel nt	insect repellent
Insel f	island
interessant	interesting
Internet-Anschluss m	internet access
Internet-Seite f	website
Ire (Irin) m/f	Irishman/woman
irgendjemand	someone
irgendwo	somewhere
irisch adj	Irish
Irland nt	Ireland
Irrtum m	mistake
Italien nt	Italy
Italiener(in) m/f	Italian
italienisch adj	Italian

J

German	English
ja	yes

German	English
Jacke f	jacket; cardigan
jagen	to hunt
Jahr nt	year
Jahrestag m	anniversary
Jahreszeit f	season
Jahrgang m	vintage
Jahrhundert nt	century
jährlich	annual; yearly
Jahrmarkt m	(fun) fair
Januar m	January
jeder	everyone
jede(r/s)	each
jemand	somebody; someone
jene	those
jetzt	now
Joghurt m	yoghurt
Johannisbeere(n) f	currant(s)
jucken	to itch
Jude/Jüdin m/f	Jew
Jugendherberge f	youth hostel

German	English
Jugendliche(r) m/f	teenager
Juli m	July
jung	young
Junge m	boy
Junggeselle m	bachelor
Juni m	June
Juwelier m	jeweller's

K

German	English
Kabelfern-sehen nt	cable TV
kabellose Internet-Verbindung f	wireless internet
Kaffee m	coffee
Kaffeehaus nt	café
Kakao m	cocoa
Kalbfleisch nt	veal
kalt	cold
Kamillentee m	camomile tea
Kamin m	fireplace
kämpfen	to fight

German – English

German – English

Kanada nt	Canada	Kastanie f	chestnut
Kanadier(in) m/f	Canadian	Kater m	hangover; tomcat
kanadisch adj	Canadian	katholisch	Catholic
Kanal m	canal; (English) Channel	Katze f	cat
kandiert	glacé	kaufen	to buy
Kaninchen nt	rabbit	Kaufhaus nt	department store
Kapelle f	chapel; orchestra	Kaugummi m	chewing gum
kaputt	broken; out of order	Kaution f	deposit
kaputtmachen	to break (object)	Kehle f	throat
Karotten pl	carrots	kein(e)...	no...
Karte f	card; ticket; map; menu	keine(r/s)	none
		Keks(e) m	biscuit(s) (sweet)
Kartentelefon nt	cardphone	Kellner(in) m/f	waiter/waitress
Kartoffel(n) f	potato(es)	kennen	to be acquainted with
Kartoffelpüree nt	mashed potato	Kern m	pip; core
Kartoffelsalat m	potato salad	Kerze f	candle
Käse m	cheese	Kette f	chain
Kasse f	cash desk	Kiefer f	jaw
Kassierer(in) m/f	cashier		

Kiefer f	pine tree		
Kind(er) nt	child(ren)		
Kinn nt	chin		
Kino nt	cinema		
Kirche f	church		
Kirmes f	funfair		
Kirsche(n) f	cherry (cherries)		
Kissen nt	cushion; pillow		
Klage f	complaint		
klar	clear		
Klarer m	schnapps		
Klasse f	class; grade		
Klavier nt	piano		
kleben	to stick (with glue)		
Kleid nt	dress		
Kleider pl	clothes		
klein	little (small); short		
Kleingeld nt	change (money)		
Klettband nt	Velcro®		

klettern	to climb (mountains)
klimatisiert	air-conditioned
klingeln	to ring (bell, phone)
Kloß m	dumpling
Kloster nt	monastery; convent
Kneipe f	pub
Knie nt	knee
Knoblauch m	garlic
Knöchel m	ankle
Knochen m	bone
Knödel m	dumpling
Koch m	chef
kochen	to boil; to cook
Köchin f	cook
Kochschinken m	cooked ham
koffeinfreier Kaffee m	decaffeinated coffee
Koffer m	suitcase; trunk

Kofferanhänger m	luggage tag
Kohl m	cabbage
Kollege (Kollegin) m/f	colleague
Köln	Cologne
komisch	funny (amusing)
kommen	to come
Komödie f	comedy
Kondensmilch f	condensed milk
Konditorei f	cake shop; café
Konferenz f	conference
Konfitüre f	jam
König m	king
Königin f	queen
königlich	royal
können	to be able to; to know how to
Konsulat nt	consulate
Kontaktlinsen pl	contact lenses
Konto nt	bank account
Kontrolle f	check; control

Konzert nt	concert
Kopf m	head
Kopfhörer pl	headphones
Kopfsalat m	lettuce
Kopfschmerzen pl	headache
kopieren	to copy
Korkenzieher m	corkscrew
Körper m	body
kosten	to cost
Kosten pl	cost (price)
kostenlos	free of charge
köstlich	delicious
Krabbe f	crab
Krämpfe pl	cramps
krank	ill; sick
Krankenhaus nt	hospital
Krankheit f	disease
Kräutertee m	herbal tea
Krebs m	crab (animal); cancer (illness)
Kreditkarte f	credit card

German - English

German	English
Kreuzfahrt f	cruise
Kreuzung f	junction; crossroads
Kreuzworträtsel nt	crossword
Krieg m	war
Küche f	kitchen; cuisine
Kuchen m	flan; cake
Kugelschreiber m	pen; biro
Kuh f	cow
kühl	cool
Kühlschrank m	fridge
Kunde (Kundin) m/f	client; customer
Kundenkarte f	store card
Kunsthalle f	art gallery
Kunsthandwerksmarkt m	craft fair
künstlich	artificial; man-made
Kurort m	spa
Kurs m	course; exchange rate
Kurve f	curve; corner; bend
kurz	short; brief
küssen	to kiss

L

German	English
lächeln	to smile
lachen	to laugh
Lachs m	salmon
Laden m	shop; store
Lamm nt	lamb
Land nt	country (Italy, France, etc); land
Landkarte f	map (of country)
Landschaft f	countryside
Landwein m	table wine
lang	long
langsam	slow(ly)
langweilig	boring
Lärm m	noise
lassen	to let (allow)
Lastwagen m	truck; lorry
Lauch m	leek
laufen	to run
Laugenbrezel f	soft pretzel
laut	noisy; loud(ly); aloud
Lebensgefahr f	danger to life
Lebensmittel pl	groceries
Lebkuchen m	gingerbread
ledig	single (not married)
leer	empty; flat (battery); blank (disk/tape)
legen	to lay
Lehrer(in) m/f	teacher (school); instructor

leicht	light (not heavy); easy	Liegestuhl m	deckchair
leid: (es) tut mir leid	(I'm) sorry	Lift m	elevator; lift
leider	unfortunately	Limone f	lime (fruit)
Leihgebühr f	rental (fee)	Linienflug m	scheduled flight
leise	quietly; soft; faint	linke(r/s)	left(-hand)
leiser stellen	to turn down (volume)	links	to the left; on the left
		Loch nt	hole
lernen	to learn	lochen	to punch (ticket, etc)
lesen	to read		
letzte(r/s)	last; final	locker	loose (screw, tooth)
Leute pl	people	Löffel m	spoon
Licht nt	light	Loge f	box (in theatre)
liebe(r)	dear (in letter)	Lohn m	wage
lieben	to love	Lokal nt	pub
liebenswürdig	kind	Lorbeerblatt nt	bayleaf
lieber	rather	los	loose
Lieblings-	favourite	was ist los?	what's wrong?
Lied nt	song	löslich	soluble
		Löwe m	lion

Luft f	air
Luftpost f	air mail
Lüge f	lie (untruth)
Lutscher m	lollipop

M

machen	to make; to do
das macht nichts	that doesn't matter
Mädchen nt	girl
Mädchenname m	maiden name
Magenschmerzen pl	stomach-ache
Magenverstimmung f	indigestion
Mai m	May
Mais m	sweetcorn
Malzbier nt	malt beer
man	one
manchmal	sometimes
Mandarine f	tangerine

German – English

German – English

German	English
Mandel f	almond; tonsil
Mandelentzündung f	tonsillitis
Mann m	man; husband
Männer pl	men
männlich	masculine; male
Mantel m	coat
mariniert	marinated
Markt m	market
Marktplatz m	market place
Marmelade f	jam
März m	March
Material nt	material
Mauer f	wall
Maut f	toll (motorway)
Medikament nt	drug; medicine
Medizin f	medicine
Meer nt	sea
Meeresfrüchte pl	seafood
Mehl nt	flour
mehr	more
Mehrwegflasche f	returnable bottle (usually with a deposit)
Mehrwertsteuer (MWST) f	value-added tax (VAT)
mein	my
meiste(n)	most
melden	to report (tell about)
Menge f	crowd
Messe f	fair (commercial); mass (church)
Messegelände nt	exhibition centre
messen	to measure
Messer nt	knife
Metzgerei f	butcher's
mich	me (direct object)
Mietauto nt	hire car
mieten	to hire; to rent (house, etc)
Mietgebühr f	rental charge
Mietvertrag m	lease (rental)
Migräne f	migraine
Milch f	milk
Milchprodukte pl	dairy produce
minderwertig	low-quality
Mindest-	minimum
Minute(n) f	minute(s)
Minze f	mint (herb)
mir	me (indirect object)
mischen	to mix
Missverständnis nt	misunderstanding
mit	with
Mitglied nt	member (of club, etc)
mitnehmen	to give a lift to
zum Mitnehmen	take-away (food)
Mittag m	midday
Mittagessen nt	lunch
Mitte f	middle

German	English
Mittel *nt*	means
ein Mittel gegen	a remedy for
mittelalterlich	medieval
Mittelmeer *nt*	Mediterranean
Mitternacht *f*	midnight
Mittwoch *m*	Wednesday
modern	fashionable; modern
mögen *(to like)*	to enjoy
möglich	possible
Möhre(n) *f*	carrot(s)
Monat *m*	month
monatlich	monthly
Mond *m*	moon
Montag *m*	Monday
Morgen *m*	morning
morgen	tomorrow
Morgendämmerung *f*	dawn
Morgenmantel *m*	dressing gown
Motorrad *nt*	motorbike
Mücke *f*	midge; fly
müde	tired
Müll *m*	rubbish
Mülleimer *m*	bin *(dustbin)*
Mülltrennung *f*	waste separation *(for recycling)*
München	Munich
Mund *m*	mouth
Münster *nt*	cathedral
Münze(n) *f*	coin(s)
Münztelefon *nt*	payphone
Muscheln *pl*	mussels
Musik *f*	music
müssen	to have to; must
mutig	brave
Mutter *f*	mother
Mütze *f*	cap *(hat)*
MWST *f*	VAT

N

German	English
nach	after
Nachbar(in) *m/f*	neighbour
Nachmittag *m*	afternoon
Nachname *m*	surname
Nachrichten *pl*	news
Nachspeise *f*	dessert; pudding
nächste(r/s)	next
Nacht *f*	night
Nachtisch *m*	dessert
nachzahlen	to pay extra
Nähe *f*	proximity
in der Nähe	nearby
Name *m*	name; surname
Nase *f*	nose
nass	wet
Naturschutzgebiet *nt*	nature reserve
Nebel *m*	mist; fog
neben	by *(next to)*; beside
neblig	foggy
Neffe *m*	nephew

German - English

German – English

nehmen	to catch (bus, train); to take (remove)
nein	no
nennen	to quote (price)
nett	nice (person); kind
Netto-	net (income, price)
neu	new
neueste(r/s)	newest; latest
Neujahr(stag) m	New Year's Day
Neuseeland nt	New Zealand
nicht	not; non-
Nichte f	niece
Nichtraucher m	non-smoker
nichts	nothing
nie	never
Niederlande pl	Netherlands
niedrig	low
niemand	no one; nobody

nirgends	nowhere
noch	still (up to this time); yet
noch ein(e)	extra (more); another
Norden m	north
Nordirland nt	Northern Ireland
nördlich	north; northern
Nordsee f	North Sea
Notarzt m	emergency doctor
Notdienst-apotheke f	on-duty chemist
Notfall m	emergency
nötig	necessary
Notruf m	emergency number
notwendig	essential; necessary
November m	November
nüchtern	sober

Nummer f	number; act
nur	only
Nürnberg	Nuremberg
Nuss (Nüsse) f	nut(s)
nützlich	useful

O

oben	upstairs; above; this side up
oben auf	on top of…
Obst nt	fruit
Obstkuchen m	fruit tart
oder	or
offen	open
offene Weine pl	wine served by the glass
öffentlich	public
öffnen	to open; to undo
Öffnungszeiten pl	business hours
oft	often
ohne	without

German	English
Ohrenschmerzen pl	earache
Oktober m	October
Onkel m	uncle
Oper f	opera
Optiker m	optician's
Orange f	orange (fruit)
Orangensaft m	orange juice
Ort m	place
örtlich	local
Osten m	east
Österreich nt	Austria
Österreicher(in) m/f	Austrian
österreichisch adj	Austrian
östlich	eastern

P

German	English
packen	to pack (luggage)
Paket nt	parcel; packet
Pampelmuse(n) f	grapefruit(s)
Panne f	breakdown (of car)
Paprikaschote f	pepper (vegetable)
Parken verboten	no parking
Parkhaus nt	multi-storey car park
Parkplatz m	car park
Parkschein m	parking ticket (to display)
Parkuhr f	parking meter
Pass m	passport; pass (in mountains)
passen	to fit
passieren	to happen
Passkontrolle f	passport control
Passnummer f	passport number
Pauschalreise f	package tour
Pauschaltarif m	flat-rate tariff
Pendelverkehr m	shuttle (service)
Pension f	boarding house; guesthouse
pensioniert	retired
Peperoni pl	chilli
perlend	sparkling
Personal nt	staff
Personalausweis m	identity card
Personalien pl	particulars
persönlich	personal(ly)
Pfand nt	deposit
Pfannkuchen m	pancake
Pfefferkuchen m	gingerbread
Pfefferminztee m	mint tea
Pferd nt	horse
Pferderennen nt	horse-racing
Pfirsich(e) m	peach(es)
Pflanze f	plant (green)
Pflaster nt	plaster (for cut)
Pflaume(n) f	plum(s)
Pforte f	gate

German – English

German – English

German	English
Pfund nt	pound
pikant	savoury
Pils/Pilsner nt	lager
Pilz(e) m	mushroom(s)
Pistazie f	pistachio
planmäßig	scheduled
Platz m	seat; space; square (in town)
Plätzchen nt	biscuit(s)
Platzkarte f	seat reservation (ticket)
plötzlich	suddenly
pochiert	poached (egg, fish)
Polen nt	Poland
Polizei f	police
Polizeirevier nt	police station
Polizeiwache f	police station
Porree m	leek
Portier m	porter (for door)

German	English
Portugal nt	Portugal
Portugiese/ Portugies-in m/f	Portuguese
portugiesisch adj	Portuguese
Post f	post office
Postamt nt	post office
Postanweisung f	money order
postlagernd	poste restante
Postleitzahl f	postcode
praktisch	handy, practical
Pralinen pl	chocolates
Praxis f	doctor's surgery
Preis m	prize; price
Preiselbeersaft m	cranberry juice
Preisliste f	price list
Privatweg m	private road
pro Stunde	per hour
pro Kopf	per person
probieren	to taste; to sample

German	English
prost!	cheers!
provisorisch	temporary
Prozent nt	per cent
prüfen	to check (oil, water, etc)
Prüfung f	exam (school, university)
Publikum nt	audience
Pullover m	sweater; jumper
Pulver nt	powder
pünktlich	on schedule; punctual
pur	straight (drink)
Pute f	turkey

Q

German	English
Qualität f	quality
Qualitätswein m	good quality wine
Quantität f	quantity

German	English
Quelle f	spring (of water); source
quetschen	to squeeze
Quittung f	receipt

R

German	English
Rabatt m	discount
Rad fahren	to cycle
Rasen m	lawn
rasieren	to shave
Rasierklinge f	razor blade
Rasierschaum m	shaving foam
Rasthof m	service area; travel inn
Rastplatz m	picnic area
Raststätte f	service area
raten	to advise
Rathaus nt	town hall
rau	rough
Rauchen verboten	no smoking
Raum m	space (room)
rechnen	to calculate
Rechnung f	bill (account); invoice
rechte(r/s)	right-hand
rechts	to the right; on the right
reden	to speak
reduziert	reduced
Reformhaus nt	health food shop
Regen m	rain
Regenschirm m	umbrella
regnen	to rain
reich	rich (person)
reichhaltig	rich (food)
reif	ripe; mature (cheese)
Reihe f	row (line); tier
rein	pure
reinigen	to clean
Reinigung f	dry-cleaner's
Reis m	rice
Reise f	trip (journey)
Reisebüro nt	travel agency
Reiseführer m	guidebook
Reisekrankheit f	travel sickness
Reisescheck m	traveller's cheque
rennen	to run
Rentner(in) m/f	pensioner; senior citizen
Reparatur f	repair
reparieren	to repair; to mend
reservieren	to book; to reserve
Reservierung f	booking; reservation
Restgeld nt	change (money)
retten	to rescue; to save (person)

German – English

German - English

German	English
Rezept *nt*	prescription; recipe
R-Gespräch *nt*	reverse charge call
Rhein *m*	Rhine
richtig	correct; right; proper
Richtung *f*	direction
riechen	to smell
Rinderbraten *m*	roast beef
Rindfleisch *nt*	beef
Ringstraße *f*	ring road
Rock *m*	skirt
Roggenbrot *nt*	rye bread
roh	raw
Roman *m*	novel
rosa	pink
Rosenkohl *m*	Brussels sprouts
Rosenmontag *m*	carnival (*Monday before Shrove Tuesday*)
Rosine(n) *f*	raisin(s)
Rostbraten *m*	roast
rostfreier Stahl *m*	stainless steel
Röstkartoffeln *pl*	sautéed potatoes
rot	red
rote Bete *f*	beetroot
rote Johannisbeeren *pl*	redcurrants
Rotwein *m*	red wine
Rückerstattung *f*	refund
Rückfahrkarte *f*	return ticket
Rückflugticket *nt*	return airticket
rückwärts	backwards
rufen	to shout
Ruhe *f*	rest (*repose*); peace (*calm*)
Ruhe!	be quiet!
ruhig	calm; quiet(ly); peaceful
Rührei *nt*	scrambled egg
rund	round
Rundfahrt *f*	tour; round trip
rutschig	slippery

S

German	English
Sachen *pl*	stuff (*things*); belongings
Sachsen *nt*	Saxony
Sackgasse *f*	cul-de-sac
Saft *m*	juice
sagen	to say; to tell (*fact, news*)
Sahne *f*	cream (*dairy*)
Saison *f*	season
Salbe *f*	ointment
Salz *nt*	salt
Salzkartoffeln *pl*	boiled potatoes
Samstag *m*	Saturday
Satellitenfernsehen *nt*	satellite TV
satt	full

German	English
Satz m	set (collection); sentence
säubern	to clean
sauer	sour
Sauerkraut nt	sauerkraut
S-Bahn f	suburban railway
Schach nt	chess
Schaden m	damage
schädlich	harmful
Schaf nt	sheep
Schaffner(in) m/f	conductor (bus, train); guard
schälen	to peel (fruit)
Schalter m	switch
scharf	hot (spicy); sharp
Schatten m	shade
schätzen	to value; to estimate
Schauer m	rain shower
Schaumwein m	sparkling wine
Schauspiel nt	play
Schauspieler(in) m/f	actor/actress
Scheck m	cheque
Scheibe f	slice
Schein(e) m	banknote(s); certificate(s)
scheinen	to shine (sun, etc); to seem
Schere f	scissors (pair of)
scherzen	to joke
Schi-	see Ski-
schicken	to send
Schild nt	sign; label
Schinken m	ham
Schlachterei f	butcher's
schlafen	to sleep
schlagen	to hit
Schlagsahne f	whipped cream
Schlange f	queue; snake
schlecht	bad; badly
schließen	to shut; to close
Schließfach nt	locker
schlimm	serious
Schlittschuh laufen	to ice skate
Schloss nt	castle; lock (on door, etc)
Schluss m	end
Schlüssel m	key
Schlüsselkarte f	cardkey (for hotel)
Schlussverkauf m	sale
schmecken	to taste
schmelzen	to melt
Schmerz m	pain; ache
schmerzhaft	painful
Schmerzmittel nt	painkiller
Schmuck m	jewellery; decorations
schmutzig	dirty
Schnee m	snow
schneiden	to cut
schnell	fast; quick

German - English

German - English

Schnellimbiss m	snack bar	
Schnittbohnen pl	green beans	
Schnittlauch m	chives	
Schnittwunde f	cut	
Schokolade f	chocolate	
schön	lovely; fine; beautiful; good (pleasant)	
Schotte (Schottin) m/f	Scot	
schottisch	Scottish	
Schottland nt	Scotland	
schrecklich	awful	
schreiben	to write	
Schreibwarenhandlung f	stationer's	
schriftlich	in writing	
Schritt fahren!	dead slow!	
Schuh(e) m	shoe(s)	
Schulden pl	debts	
Schule f	school	

Schuppen pl	scales (of fish); dandruff
schwach	weak
Schwager m	brother-in-law
Schwägerin f	sister-in-law
schwanger	pregnant
schwarz	black
Schwarzbrot nt	brown bread
schwarze Johannisbeeren pl	blackcurrants
Schwarzweißfilm m	black and white film
Schweinefleisch nt	pork
Schweiß m	sweat
Schweiz f	Switzerland
Schweizer(in) m/f	Swiss
schweizerisch adj	Swiss
schwer	heavy
Schwester f	sister; nurse; nun
Schwiegermutter f	mother-in-law
Schwiegersohn m	son-in-law

Schwiegertochter f	daughter-in-law
Schwiegervater m	father-in-law
schwierig	hard (difficult)
Schwimmbad nt	swimming pool
schwimmen	to swim
schwind(e)lig	dizzy
schwitzen	to sweat
See f	sea
See m	lake
seekrank	seasick
segeln	to sail
sehen	to see
Sehenswürdigkeit f	sight; attraction
sehr	very
seicht	shallow (water)
Seide f	silk
Seife f	soap
sein(e)	his
sein	to be
seit	since

Seite *f*	page; side
Seitenstreifen *m*	hard shoulder
Sekretär(in) *m/f*	secretary
Sekt *m*	sparkling wine
Sekunde *f*	second (time)
Selbstbedienung *f*	self-service
Sellerie *m*	celery
selten	rare (unique)
seltsam	strange (odd)
Senf *m*	mustard
September *m*	September
servieren	to serve (food)
setzen	to place; to put
sich setzen	to sit down
setzen Sie sich bitte	please take a seat
sicher	sure; safe; definite
Sicherheit *f*	safety
Sicherheitsgurt *m*	seatbelt; safety belt
Sicherheitskontrolle *f*	security check
sie	she; they
Sie	you (formal singular and plural)
singen	to sing
sitzen	to sit
Ski fahren	to ski
SMS *f*	text message
eine SMS schreiben	to text
Sodbrennen *nt*	heartburn
sofort	at once; immediately
Sohn *m*	son
Sojabohnen *pl*	soya beans
Sommer *m*	summer
Sommerferien *pl*	summer holidays
Sonderangebot *nt*	special offer
sonn- und feiertags	Sundays and public holidays
Sonnabend *m*	Saturday
Sonne *f*	sun
Sonnenaufgang *m*	sunrise
Sonnenbrand *m*	sunburn
Sonnenbräune *f*	suntan
Sonnenbrille *f*	sunglasses
Sonnenstich *m*	sunstroke
Sonnenuntergang *m*	sunset
sonnig	sunny
Sonntag *m*	Sunday
sorgen für	to look after; to take care of
Soße *f*	dressing; sauce
Spanien *nt*	Spain
Spanier(in) *m/f*	Spaniard

German – English

German – English

German	English
spanisch *adj*	Spanish
sparen	to save (money)
Spargel *m*	asparagus
Sparpreis *m*	economy fare
Spaß *m*	fun; joke
spät	late
Spaziergang *m*	stroll; walk
Speck *m*	bacon
Speicherkarte *f*	memory card
Speise *f*	dish; food
Speisekarte *f*	menu
Spesen *pl*	expenses
Spezialität *f*	speciality
Spiegelei *nt*	fried egg
Spiel *nt*	game; pack (of cards)
spielen	to gamble; to play
Spinat *m*	spinach
Sprache *f*	speech; language

German	English
sprechen	to speak
sprechen mit	to talk to
Sprechstunde *f*	surgery (hours of opening)
sprudelnd	fizzy
Sprudelwasser *nt*	sparkling water
Spucktüte *f*	sick bag
spülen	to flush toilet; to rinse
Spur *f*	lane (of motorway/main road)
Staatsange-hörigkeit *f*	nationality
Stadion *nt*	stadium
Stadt *f*	town; city
ständig	permanent(ly); continuous(ly)
stark	strong
statt	instead of
stattfinden	to take place

German	English
Stau *m*	traffic jam
Staub *m*	dust
stechen	to bite (insect)
Stechmücke *f*	mosquito; gnat
Steckrübe *f*	turnip
stehen	to stand
stehlen	to steal
steil	steep
Stelle *f*	job; place; point (in space)
sterben	to die
Stern *m*	star
Steuer *f*	tax
Stich *m*	bite (by insect); stitch (sewing); sting
Stiefel *pl*	boots (long)
Stiefmutter *f*	stepmother
Stiefvater *m*	stepfather
Stil *m*	style

German	English
still	still (motion(less)); quiet
stilles Wasser nt	still water
Stimme f	voice
stimmt so!	keep the change!
Stirn f	forehead
Stockwerk nt	storey
Stoff m	cloth (fabric)
stören	to disturb (interrupt)
Stornierung f	cancellation
Störung f	hold-up; fault; medical disorder
stoßen	to knock; to push
Stoßzeit f	rush hour
Strafe f	punishment; fine
Strafzettel m	parking ticket (fine)
Strand m	beach
Straße f	road; street
Straße gesperrt	road closed
Straßenarbeiten pl	roadworks
Straßenbahn f	tram
Straßenkarte f	road map
Streifenkarte f	multiple journey travelcard
streiten	to quarrel
Strickjacke f	cardigan
Strumpfhose f	tights
Stück nt	bit; piece
Studentenermäßigung f	student discount
Stufe f	step (stair)
Stuhl m	chair
stumpf	blunt (blade)
Stunde f	hour; lesson
Sturm m	storm
suchen	to look for
Suchmaschine f	search engine
Süden m	south
südlich	southern
Summe f	sum (total amount)
Suppe f	soup
süß	sweet
Süßigkeiten pl	sweets
Süßstoff m	sweetener; saccharin
Süßwaren pl	confectionery

T

German	English
Tafelwein m	table wine
Tag m	day
jeden Tag	every day
Tagespauschale f	daily unlimited rate
Tagessuppe f	soup of the day
täglich	daily
Tal nt	valley

German – English

German	English
Tanne f	fir
Tante f	aunt
tanzen	to dance
Tasche f	pocket; bag
Taschenbuch nt	paperback
Taschendieb m	pickpocket
Taschenrechner m	calculator
Taschentuch nt	handkerchief
Tasse f	cup
Taube f	pigeon
Tauchen nt	diving
tauschen	to exchange
Tee m	tea
Teebeutel m	tea bag
Teekanne f	teapot
Teelöffel m	teaspoon
Teil m/nt	part
teilen	to divide; to share
Telefonauskunft f	directory enquiries
Telefonbuch nt	phone directory
telefonieren	to telephone
Telefonzelle f	phonebox
Teller m	plate
Termin m	date; deadline; appointment
Terminal m	terminal (airport)
teuer	dear (expensive)
Theke f	counter (in shop, bar, etc)
Thunfisch m	tuna
tief	deep; low (in pitch)
Tiefkühltruhe f	deep freeze; freezer
Tier nt	animal
Tintenfisch m	octopus; squid
Tisch m	table
Tischwein m	table wine
Toastbrot nt	sliced white bread for toasting
Tochter f	daughter
Tochtergesellschaft f	subsidiary
Tollwut f	rabies
Tomate f	tomato
Tor nt	gate; goal (sport)
Törtchen nt	cake (small)
Torte f	gâteau; tart
tot	dead
töten	to kill
Touristenklasse f	economy class
tragbar	portable
tragen	to carry; to wear
trampen	to hitchhike
Trauben pl	grapes
traurig	sad
treffen	to meet
Treppe f	stairs

German	English
Tresor m	safe
trinken	to drink
Trinkgeld nt	tip (for waiter, etc)
Trinkwasser nt	drinking water
trocken	dry; stale (bread)
Trockenmilch f	powdered milk
Trockenobst nt	dried fruit
trocknen	to dry
Truthahn m	turkey
Tschechien nt	Czech Republic
tschüs(s)	cheerio; bye
tun	to do
Tunfisch m	tuna
Tür f	door
Turm m	tower
Turnschuhe pl	gym shoes
typisch	typical

U

German	English
u.A.w.g.	RSVP
U-Bahn f	metro; underground
übel	sick (nauseous); bad
über	over; above; about; via
überall	everywhere
überbuchen	to overbook
Überfall m	mugging
überfällig	overdue
überfüllt	crowded (train, shop, etc)
Übergewicht nt	excess baggage; overweight
überhitzen	to overheat
überholen	to overtake
Übernachtung mit Frühstück	bed and breakfast
überprüfen	to check (to examine)
übersetzen	to translate
überweisen	to transfer (money)
übrig	left over; extra (spare)
Uhr f	clock; watch
um	around
um 4 Uhr	at 4 o'clock
umdrehen	to turn around
umsonst	free (costing nothing)
umsteigen	to change
Umwelt f	environment
unbegrenzt	unlimited
und	and
Unfall m	accident
ungefähr	approximately
ungefährlich	safe (not dangerous)
ungewöhnlich	unusual
ungültig	invalid

German – English

German – English

German	English
unmöglich	impossible; unsafe
uns	us
unsere(e)	our
unsicher	uncertain (fact)
unten	downstairs; under(neath); below
unter	
unterbrechen	to interrupt
Unterführung f	subway
Unterkunft f	accommodation
unterrichten	to teach
Unterschrift f	signature
Untertitel pl	subtitles
unwohl	unwell
Urlaub m	leave; holiday
Ursprungsland nt	country of origin

V

German	English
Vanillesoße f	custard
Vater m	father
Verbindung f	connection (train, etc); service (bus, etc); line (phone)
verboten	forbidden
verbringen	to spend (time)
verderben	to go bad (food); to spoil
verdienen	to deserve; to earn
verdorben	bad (fruit, vegetables)
Verein m	society (club)
vereinbaren	to agree upon; to arrange
Vereinigtes Königreich nt	United Kingdom
Vereinigte Staaten (von Amerika) pl	United States (of America)
Verfallsdatum nt	expiry date; eat-by date
Vergangenheit f	past
vergeben	to forgive; to allocate
vergessen	to forget
Vergewaltigung f	rape
Vergnügen nt	enjoyment; pleasure
Vergrößerung f	enlargement
verheiratet	married
verhindern	to prevent
Verkauf m	sale
verkaufen	to sell
Verkäufer(in) m/f	salesman/woman
Verkehr m	traffic
verkehrt	wrong
verlängern	extend (stay); renew (visa)

German	English
Verleih *m*	rental company; hire company
verletzen	to injure
verlieren	to lose
verlobt	engaged (*to be married*)
verloren	lost (*object*)
vermeiden	to avoid
vermieten	to rent; to let (*room, house*)
vermisst	missing (*person*)
verpassen	to miss (*plane, train, etc*)
verschieben	to postpone
verschiedene	several; different
verschmutzt	polluted
verschwinden	to disappear
verschwunden	missing
versichert sein	to be insured
Versicherung *f*	insurance
Verspätung *f*	delay
versprechen	to promise
verstecken	to hide
verstehen	to understand
versuchen	to try
Vertrag *m*	contract
Verwandte(r) *m/f*	relative
verwenden	to use
Verzeihung!	sorry; excuse me
verzollen	to declare goods (*customs*)
viel	much
viele	many
vielleicht	perhaps
Viertel *nt*	quarter
Viertelstunde *f*	quarter of an hour
Visitenkarte *f*	business card
Visum *nt*	visa
Vogel *m*	bird
Volkslied *nt*	folk song
voll	full
Vollkornbrot *nt*	dark rye bread; wholemeal bread
Vollmilchschokolade *f*	milk chocolate
Vollpension *f*	full board
vollständig	whole
von	from; of
vor	before; in front of
voraus	ahead
vorbei	past
vorbereiten	to prepare
Vorbestellung *f*	reservation
Vorname *m*	first name
Vorschrift *f*	regulation (*rule*)
Vorsicht *f*	caution
Vorspeise *f*	starter (*in meal*); hors d'œuvre
Vorstellung *f*	performance
Vorverkauf *m*	advance booking

German – English

German	English
Vorwahl-(nummer) f	dialling code
vorziehen	to prefer
W	
wach	awake
Wache f	security guard
Wahl f	choice; election
wählen	to dial (number); to choose
Wählton m	dialling tone
während	while; during
Währung f	currency
Wald m	wood; forest
Wales nt	Wales
Waliser(in) m/f	Welshman/woman
walisisch	Welsh
Walnuss(-nüsse) f	walnut(s)
wandern	to hike

German	English
Wanderung f	hike
wann?	when?
warm	warm
Warnung f	warning
warten (auf)	to wait (for)
Wartesaal m	waiting room
warum?	why?
was?	what?
waschbar	washable
waschen	to wash
Wasser nt	water
wasserdicht	waterproof
Wassermelone f	water melon
Wasserskifahren nt	to water ski
Wechsel m	change (small coins)
Wechselgeld nt	change
Wechselkurs m	exchange rate
wechseln	to change (money); to give change

German	English
Wechselstube f	bureau de change
Weckruf m	alarm call
Weg m	path; way; country lane
weggehen	to leave (on foot)
weh tun	to ache; to hurt (be painful)
weiblich	female; feminine
weich	soft
gekochtes Ei nt	soft-boiled egg
Weihnachten nt	Christmas
weil	because
Wein m	wine
Weinberg m	vineyard
Weinbrand m	brandy
weinen	to cry (weep)
Weinprobe f	wine-tasting
Weintrauben pl	grapes
weiß	white

German	English
Weißbrot nt	white bread
weit	far; loose (clothing)
weiter	farther; further on
weitermachen	to continue
Weizen m	wheat
welche(r/s)	which; what; which one
Welt f	world
Wende f	U-turn (in car)
wenden	to turn
wenig	little
weniger	less
wenn	if; when (with present tense)
wer?	who?
werden	to become
Werktag m	weekday
Wert m	value
Wertsachen pl	valuables
wertvoll	valuable
wesentlich	essential
Wespe f	wasp
wessen?	whose?
westlich	western
Wetter nt	weather
Wetterbericht m	weather forecast
Wettervorhersage f	weather forecast
wichtig	important
wie	like; how
wie viel?	how much?
wie viele?	how many?
wieder	again
wiederholen	to repeat
Wien	Vienna
willkommen	welcome
Wind m	wind
windig	windy
Winter m	winter
wir	we
wirksam	effective (remedy, etc)
wissen	to know (facts)
Witz m	joke
wo?	where?
Woche f	week
Wochenende nt	weekend
Wochentag m	weekday
wöchentlich	weekly
woher?	where from?
wohin?	where to?
wohnen	to stay; to live (reside)
Wohnort m	home address
Wohnung f	flat (apartment)
Wohnzimmer nt	living room
wolkig	cloudy
Wolle f	wool
wollen	to want (wish for)
Wort nt	word
Wörterbuch nt	dictionary

German – English

German – English

German	English
Wurst f	sausage
Würstchenbude f	hot-dog stand
würzig	spicy
Y	
Yachthafen m	marina
Z	
zäh	tough (meat)
Zahl f	number (figure)
zahlen	to pay
z. B.	e.g.
Zeichentrickfilm m	cartoon
Zeichnung f	drawing
zeigen	to show
Zeit f	time
Zeitkarte f	season ticket
Zeitschrift f	magazine
Zeitung f	newspaper
Zentrum nt	centre
ziehen	pull
Ziel nt	destination; goal; target
ziemlich	quite (rather)
Zimmer nt	room (in house, hotel)
Zimmer frei	vacancies
Zitrone f	lemon
Zoll m	customs/toll
zollfrei	duty-free
zornig	angry
zu	to; off; too; at
zu Hause	at home
zubereiten	to prepare
Zucker m	sugar
zuckerfrei	sugar-free
Zug m	train
zuhören	to listen
Zukunft f	future
zum Beispiel	for example
Zuname m	surname
zurück	back
zurücklassen	to leave behind
zusammen	together
zusätzlich	extra; additional
zuschauen	to watch
Zuschlag m	surcharge; supplement
Zustellung f	delivery (of mail)
Zutaten pl	ingredients
Zutritt verboten	no entry
zu viel	too much
zu viel berechnen	to overcharge
zuzüglich	extra
zweimal	twice
zweite(r/s)	second
Zwillinge pl	twins
zwischen	between
Zwischenlandung f	stopover (plane)

Further titles in Collins' phrasebook range
Collins Gem Phrasebook

Also available as **Phrasebook CD Pack**
Other titles in the series

Collins Phrasebook & Dictionary

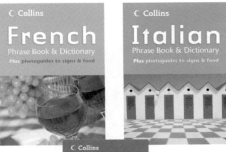

Also available as **Phrasebook CD Pack**
Other titles in the series
German Japanese Portuguese Spanish

Collins Easy: Photo Phrasebook

Also available as
Phrasebook
CD Pack

Other titles
in the series
Easy French
Easy Greek
Easy Italian